NO EASY VICTORIES

Books by John W. Gardner

NO
EASY
VICTORIES

by John W. Gardner

EDITED BY Helen Rowan

HARPER & ROW, PUBLISHERS

NEW YORK, EVANSTON, AND LONDON

1817

LIBRARY OF CONGRESS CATALOG CARD NUMBER: 68–19103

F-S

For Stephanie and Francesca

CONTENTS

ACKNOWLEDGMENTS

Helen Rowan did an extraordinarily skillful job in editing this book. We began with the idea of bringing together my articles, speeches and other writings that had not yet appeared in book form. But each piece had been prepared originally for a specific occasion or purpose, and each contained some material that was either dated or otherwise unsuitable. Helen Rowan proposed that we eliminate the unsuitable material and use only excerpts, and she did most of the work of selecting and arranging those excerpts. I am deeply indebted to her.

I am grateful to Caryl P. Haskins and Harold R. Levy for reading the manuscript, to Mrs. Velma Walters for typing and proofing it, and to Irving Goldberg and Elsa Porter for valued help on some of the pieces that went into the book.

Acknowledgment is made to *Reader's Digest* and *Life* for permission to use materials previously published by them.

INTRODUCTION

WHEN a high government official leaves office and publishes a book, the gossip columnists order advance copies. But this is not the inside story of my years in government. Nor is it a systematic statement of my position on the issues, legislative and other, which arose during those years. The full account of my position on all such matters is lodged in the reports of Congressional hearings and in official memoranda. Anyone who is interested may turn to those sources for a boring but comprehensive record of my views on education, health, welfare, family planning, civil rights, air pollution, cigarettes and cancer, juvenile delinquency and a thousand other issues.

Men intensely engaged in the action of the world probably shouldn't write books at all. They haven't time to do the job as it ought to be done—drafting, reflecting, doing further research on special topics, tearing up chapters, rewriting, and giving the whole manuscript a distinctive form and shape.

I have not done that. With the invaluable help of Helen Rowan, I have put together a collection of excerpts from my speeches and writings. They are reflections in the course of an active life. Most of the sentences in this book were written in the course of busy days and nights—in taxicabs, airplanes and hotel rooms, on weekends and holidays or late at night.

That may explain some of the book's inadequacies and some of its strengths.

One of its inadequacies is the range of subject matter. Made up as it is of pieces drafted in the interstices of action, it is tied to the events of my life and reflects my preoccupation with certain problems. The resulting gaps are obvious, as in the case of international affairs. I have been deeply troubled, as have most Americans, by developments on the international scene. I have spoken of them from time to time, but my comments do not add up to a significant contribution to this difficult subject. The plain truth is that for the past several years I have been wholly absorbed in the domestic scene.

On some of the matters covered in this book my views are best expressed by passages from my two books *Excellence* and *Self-Renewal,* and I have not hesitated to include such passages where relevant.

The reader will understand the book better and perhaps enjoy it more if he keeps in mind that it is a collection of excerpts rather than a continuous exposition. He can dip in at almost any point and quickly pick up the thread of the discourse.

NO EASY VICTORIES

CHAPTER I

TASKS FOR

THE TOUGH-MINDED

ONCE it was thought that the woes of this world were immutable—ordained by God or an inscrutable Nature, or simply a part of the unchanging order of things.

But for the past three centuries man has gained increasing confidence, justified or not, that he can have a hand in determining his own fate, can rid himself of at least some of the ancient afflictions.

Whatever else the consequences, that shift places a very heavy burden on man and his institutions. The man who once cursed his fate, now curses himself—and pays his psychoanalyst. Quite a few bright people have noted that anxiety is the price of being one's own guardian angel.

Social institutions, particularly political ones, have felt the full impact of the new attitudes. What had been a fervent prayer to an unseen Deity becomes an angry shout at political and institutional leaders.

The pressures and strains on institutions are particularly severe when people who have suffered oppression, as have some of our minority groups, begin to see the chance for a better life.

Once the grip of tradition or apathy or oppression has been broken and people can hope for such a life, their aspirations rise very steeply. But the institutions that must satisfy those aspirations change at the same old glacial speed.

As things stand now, modern man believes—at least with half his mind—that his institutions can accomplish just about anything. The fact that they fall very far short of that goal is due, he believes, to the prevalence of people who love power or money more than they love mankind.

To my mind there is an appealing (or appalling) innocence to that view. I have had ample opportunity to observe the diverse institutions of this society—the colleges and universities, the military services, business corporations, foundations, professions, government agencies and so on. And I must report that even excellent institutions run by excellent human beings are inherently sluggish, *not* hungry for innovation, *not* quick to respond to human need, *not* eager to reshape themselves to meet the challenge of the times.

I am not suggesting a polarity between men and their institutions—men eager for change, their institutions blocking it. The institutions are run by men. And often those who appear most eager for change oppose it most stubbornly when their own institutions are involved. I give you the university professor, a great friend of change provided it doesn't affect the patterns of academic life. His motto is "Innovate away from home."

We are going to have to do a far more imaginative and

aggressive job of renewing, redesigning and revitalizing our institutions if we are to meet the requirements of today.

Just as the resistant character of institutions blocks constructive change, so does lack of resources. The over-all limit on resources available to government programs is determined not just by the economy, not just by the rational and technical processes of budgeting, but by the perception on the part of Congress and the public of what needs doing and how badly it needs doing, by the willingness of the public to let itself be taxed for relevant purposes, by the courage of the Administration in calling for taxes and of the Congress in enacting them.

I believe we are now in a situation in which the gravest consequences for this nation will ensue if we fail to act decisively on the problems of the cities, poverty and discrimination. The human misery in the ghettos is not a figment of the imagination; it can be read in the statistics on infant mortality, in the crime statistics, in the unemployment figures, in the data on educational retardation. We must deal responsively and not punitively with human need.

But the resources available to cope with these problems will be determined by public awareness of the need, by the subtleties of public mood and by Congressional action. At this writing, it does not seem to me that either the Congress or the public is fully aware of the alarming character of our domestic crisis.

We are in deep trouble as a people. And history is not going to deal kindly with a rich nation that will not tax itself to cure its miseries.

The modern belief that man's institutions can accomplish just about anything he wants, when he wants it, leads to certain characteristic contemporary phenomena.

One is the bitterness and anger toward our institutions that well up when high hopes turn sour. No observer of the modern scene has failed to note the prevalent cynicism concerning all leaders, all officials, all social institutions. That cynicism is continually fed and renewed by the rage of people who expected too much in the first place and got too little in the end.

The aspirations are healthy. But soaring hope followed by rude disappointment is a formula for trouble. Leaders arise whose whole stock in trade is to exploit first the aspirations and then the disappointment. They profit on both the ups and downs of the market.

The roller coaster of aspiration and disillusionment is amusing to the extreme conservative, who thought the aspirations were silly in the first place. It gives satisfaction to the left-wing nihilist, who thinks the whole system should be brought down. It is a gold mine for mountebanks willing to promise anything and exploit any emotion. But it is a devastating whipsaw for serious and responsible leaders.

All of this leaves us with some crucial and puzzling questions of public policy. How can we make sluggish institutions more responsive to human need and the requirements of change? How can we mobilize the resources to meet the grave crises ahead?

How can we preserve our aspirations (without which no social betterment is possible) and at the same time develop the toughness of mind and spirit to face the fact that there are no easy victories?

How can we make people understand that if they expect all good things instantly, they will destroy everything? How do we tell them that they must keep unrelenting pressure on their social institutions to accomplish beneficial change but must not, in a fit of rage, destroy those institutions? How can we caution them against exploitative leaders, leaders lustful for power or for the spotlight, leaders caught in their own vanity or emotional instability, leaders selling extremist ideologies?

How can we diminish the resort to violence? Violence cannot build a better society. No society can live in constant and destructive tumult. Either we will have a civil order in which discipline is internalized in the breast of each free and responsible citizen, or sooner or later we will have repressive measures designed to re-establish order. The anarchist plays into the hands of the authoritarian. Those of us who find authoritarianism repugnant have a duty to speak out against all who destroy civil order. The time has come when the full weight of community opinion should be felt by those who break the peace or coerce through mob action.

Dissent is an element of dynamism in our system. It is good that men should expect much of their institutions, good that their aspirations for improvement of this society should be ardent.

But those elements of dynamism must have their stabilizing counterparts. One is a tough-minded recognition that the fight for a better world is a long one, a recognition that retains high hopes but immunizes against childish collapse or destructive rage in the face of disappointment. The other is an unswerving commitment to keep the public peace.

And we need something else. An increasing number of bright and able people must become involved in the development of public policy. Ours is a difficult and exhilarating form of government—not for the faint of heart, not for the tidy-minded, and in these days of complexity not for the stupid. We need men and women who can bring to government the highest order of intellect, social motivations sturdy enough to pursue good purposes despite setbacks, and a resilience of spirit equal to the frustrations of public life.

We face the gravest difficulties in the days ahead. But if we could bring to bear on our toughest problems all the talent and resources of this nation, we could accomplish some things that would leave an indelible mark on the history books.

CHAPTER II

THE PUBLIC MOOD

IN THE EARLY YEARS of this Republic, our people had wonderfully high hopes for the new nation. It was to be a model for all mankind, a city on a hill, a haven of liberty and reason and justice.

Today we are unrivaled in wealth and power. We have all the outward signs of success. What of the dream?

I don't think anyone would deny that we are uneasy in our years of triumph. Do I need to recite the list of worries—racial strife, poverty in the midst of plenty, urban decay, crime, alienation, drugs and so on and on?

But we could discuss those items fairly exhaustively without ever getting to the sources of uneasiness for many Americans today, an uneasiness that draws its strength not from any one problem but from all, an uneasiness that goes directly to the question of where we are headed, of our health and soundness as a society, and of the relationship between the individual and society.

It is a vast and complex society. It's hard to know where

you fit in—if indeed you do fit in. It's hard to identify anything you can call your community. It's hard to say who your leaders are—if there are any leaders in an intricately organized society. It's hard to feel any responsibility for what happens, or to feel any pride if things happen well, or to know what to do about it when they don't happen well.

Time-honored institutions are turning into something other than what they were; time-honored ways of thinking are changing.

In a world caught in nerve-racking tensions, a world in which modern communications keep us continuously informed of all the folly, tragedy and danger that the great globe can offer, we all live with an undercurrent of anxiety.

And the anxiety seeks an outlet. As the pressure rises, we feel a need to strike out, to fix the blame, to find a villain. It isn't easy to accept the fact that the world's ills are complex in origin, and that part of what is wrong is in our own hearts and minds.

The possibility of coherent community action is diminished today by the deep mutual suspicions and antagonisms among various groups in our national life.

As these antagonisms become more intense, the pathology is much the same whether the group involved is made up of Black Power advocates, rioting students, rural right-wingers, urban radicals or Southern segregationists. The ingredients are, first, a deep conviction on the part of the group as to its own limitless virtue or the overriding sanctity of its cause; second, grave doubts concerning the moral integrity of all others; third, a chronically aggrieved feeling that power has fallen into the hands of the unworthy (that is, the hands of others).

Every informed American knows how widely scattered are those seeds of civic disintegration. We have all heard the conversations where hatred is just beneath the surface. We have all listened to the arguments in which difference of opinion becomes defined in terms of unalterable good and evil. We have heard the degrading characterizations of those with whom one disagrees. We have listened to the bigotry of the conservative and the bigotry of the liberal. We have all observed the steady drop in the level of discourse and behavior.

Political extremism involves two prime ingredients: an excessively simple diagnosis of the world's ills and a conviction that there are identifiable villains back of it all. Such extremism comes easily to men who have doped themselves with delusions of their own unblemished virtue and the rascality of others. Blind belief in one's cause and a low view of the morality of other Americans—these seem mild failings. But they are the soil in which ranker weeds take root—political lunacy, terrorism, and the deep, destructive cleavages that paralyze a society.

There used to be only a few chronically angry people in our national life. Today all seem caught up in mutual recriminations—Negro and white, rich and poor, conservative and liberal, hawk and dove, Democrat and Republican, labor and management, North and South, young and old.

Extremists of the right and the left work with purposeful enthusiasm to deepen our suspicion and fear of one another and to loosen the bonds that hold the society together. The trouble, of course, is that they may succeed in pulling the society apart. And will anyone really know how to put it together again?

The cohesiveness of a society, the commitment of large numbers of people to live together and work together, is a fairly mysterious thing. We don't know what makes it happen. If it breaks down, we don't know how we might go about repairing it.

This is a moment when we are acutely aware of our problems—so much so that people who are naturally melancholy or pessimistic or easily defeated find the awareness almost more than they can bear. But I can't think that we were better off when we were less aware of our problems.

We have the feeling that the problems are getting graver by the minute, and we read searing indictments of our society by social critics who share the generally heightened consciousness. But the problems aren't getting worse, and we're not any more guilty than we were twenty or fifty or a hundred years ago. In fact, we're better off, if only because problems pulled to the surface and argued about are less malignant than problems suppressed or ignored.

There are a lot of ways of misunderstanding the world and what goes on in it. I marvel at the variety.

One way is to stuff all the new problems into old categories and then think about them in old, comfortable ways.

The people who do this inevitably ask the wrong questions, which means they get the wrong answers.

Another short cut to a sense of futility is to become so preoccupied with the gossip, personalities, feuds and episodes of the moment that one never looks at a deeper issue straight on. To be honest, I am shocked at the prevalence of this approach today. A lot of people who should know better are indulging their taste for pettiness and feeding on trivia. It's a thin diet.

And there's still another kind of person who manages to misjudge the world and winds up fatigued. He believes that what is wrong is obvious, and that the solutions are equally obvious. In his view, the only reason we don't achieve instant Utopia is that evil or stupid people are blocking the way. He takes a world full of challenging problems and transforms it into a world full of reprehensible people.

The middle-of-the-road American is like a preoccupied king: he doesn't react readily, but once aroused he rules the nation.

He doesn't comprehend all the complexities of modern life—who does?—but he comprehends some things that are crucial to the strength and stability of the nation, among them the simple claims of responsibility.

Both extremes of the political spectrum are characterized by irresponsibility. The middle-of-the-road American—Negro or white—has put up with a lot from the extremists. He's about ready for a Revolt of Common Sense.

CHAPTER III

THE AMERICAN COMMITMENT

I BELIEVE that large numbers of Americans—and I count myself among them—have in recent years come to some kind of decision as to the sort of society they really want.

We found ourselves in a period of unprecedented affluence, and we decided that affluence wasn't enough. We found ourselves in a period of extraordinary technical achievements, and we decided that technical proficiency wasn't enough.

We decided that what we really wanted was a society designed for people:

- a society in which every young person could fulfill the promise that was in him;
- a society in which every person, old or young, could live his life with some measure of dignity;
- a society in which ignorance and disease and want would tyrannize no longer;
- a society of opportunity and fulfillment.

I'm speaking of something that has happened fairly recently, but these are not new themes in our national life. They represent a rebirth, a rededication to values that were always at the heart of the American commitment.

Unfortunately, some of our fellow citizens do not honor those ends. But many others do. Many live by the American commitment and live to further that commitment.

It can be honored only by deeds. If we say one thing and do another, then we are dealers in illusions and not a great people.

No one should underestimate the great scope and difficulty of the tasks we are undertaking (and by "we" I mean people in and out of government)—the elimination of poverty, the redesign of our cities, the drastic upgrading of state and local government, the creation of a genuinely humane environment for older Americans, the raising of our schools to a new level of quality.

All of these tasks are complex, most are costly, some are painful. They cannot be accomplished without a great burst of energy and concern on the part of millions of Americans.

I believe that such concern and commitment will be forthcoming when enough Americans realize how intimately our current efforts are tied to the basic values that give meaning and continuity to our life as a people.

Basic to any widespread release of human potential are equality of opportunity and equal access to the benefits of the society.

Every child should enjoy the advantages that make healthy growth and development possible. The avenues of individual fulfillment should be open to everyone. No one should be shut out from the life of the society.

It is an ideal to which we have been grievously unfaithful.

The idea of the worth and dignity of the individual is thousands of years old. But embedding that idea in social and political institutions has been a painfully slow process. It is still slow.

Our own history is instructive. No nation had ever before expressed so clear a concern for individual freedom and fulfillment as was expressed in our founding documents.

Yet it was not until 1863 that we freed the slaves. It was not until the early years of this century that we outlawed child labor. It was not until 1920 that women were allowed to vote. It was not until 1954 that the Supreme Court outlawed segregation in the schools. And degrading poverty and discrimination still exist in this free and prosperous land.

Don't let anyone tell you we're confused. We know the values to which we are being unfaithful. You may ask, "What difference does it make that we agree on our values if we aren't faithful to them?" I would answer that from the standpoint of therapy it always makes a difference what the patient is suffering from. This patient is not suffering from confusion but from infidelity.

Back of every great civilization, behind all the panoply of power and wealth, is something as powerful as it is insubstantial: a set of ideas, attitudes, convictions and the confidence that those ideas and convictions are viable.

No nation can achieve greatness unless it believes in

something—and unless that something has the moral dimensions to sustain a great civilization.

If the light of belief flickers out, then all the productive capacity and all the know-how and all the power of the nation will be as nothing, and the darkness will gather.

In Guatemala and southern Mexico one can observe the Indians who are without doubt the lineal descendants of those who created the Mayan civilization. Today they are a humble people, not asking much of themselves or the world, and not getting much. A light went out.

The geography and natural resources are virtually unchanged; the genetic make-up of the people is no doubt much the same. They were once a great people. Now they do not even remember their greatness. What happened?

I suspect that in the case of the Mayans the ruling ideas were too primitive to sustain a great civilization for long.

What about our own ideas? Can they sustain a great civilization?

The answer depends on what ideas we are talking about. Americans have valued and sought and believed in many different things: freedom, power, money, equality, justice, technology, bigness, success, comfort, speed, peace, war, discipline, freedom from discipline and so on.

I like to believe that most Americans would agree on which of those values might serve as the animating ideas for a great civilization, but it's not my intention to review here the moral undergirding of our society.

I deal with a side of American society in which the existence of certain ruling ideals is visible and inescapable. I see children being taught, the sick healed, the aged cared for, the crippled rehabilitated, the talented nurtured and developed, the mentally ill treated, the weak strengthened.

Those tasks are not done by unbelieving people. I believe that when we are being most true to ourselves as Americans we are seeking a society in which every young person has the opportunity to grow to his full stature in every way, a society in which no one is irreparably damaged by circumstances that can be prevented.

The release of human potential, the enhancement of individual dignity, the liberation of the human spirit—those are the deepest and truest goals to be conceived by the hearts and minds of the American people.

And those are ideas that can sustain and strengthen a great civilization—if we believe in them, if we are honest about them, if we have the courage and stamina to live for them.

Such ideas cannot be said to be alive unless they live in the acts of men. We must build them into our laws and our institutions and our ways of dealing with one another. That is slow, arduous, painful work, and you don't get many cheers while you're doing it.

But it is the great work of our generation. Each preceding generation had its great work to perform—founding the nation, conquering the wilderness, settling the land. Ours is to make this a livable society for every American.

CHAPTER IV

A JUST SOCIETY

Our gravest domestic problem today has to do with the role of the Negro in American life. The central cities of our great metropolitan areas are becoming almost wholly Negro communities. Conflict between the races is increasing. If we find no way of reversing the trend, we will end up with two nations, with an embittered and angry nation within a nation, with two peoples who don't know each other, don't mingle, and meet only to vent their hostility.

The problem of justice for the Negro has gnawed on the national conscience ever since this nation was founded. It is, in an important sense, *the* American problem. If any problem is especially and peculiarly ours, with roots in our history and scars in our memory, this is it.

No other modern problem touches more profoundly the values we profess to cherish. And history has handed our generation the task of solving it.

Everything we believe in, the phrases in our founding documents, the words on the monuments, say that every individual is of value. Our record of dealing with Negro Americans says something very different. A confrontation was bound to come, and it has come in this generation. It will not be resolved by violence or hatred or bitterness or police suppression. It will only be resolved by patient, determined efforts on the part of the great, politically moderate, majority of whites and Negroes.

All who are concerned with civil rights are impatient with our progress, and rightly so. All who care about the quality of American life and the future of our democracy *must* be impatient, for until we achieve justice for the Negro American, we cannot rest easy. We cannot speak of American ideals with a clear conscience; we cannot call this the land of opportunity without a troubled heart.

What we have now is a recipe for disaster:

- grossly inadequate education for the majority of Negro youngsters and living conditions that will surely perpetuate their handicaps;
- gross job discrimination against Negroes on the part of many labor unions and others;
- conditions in the ghettos that breed crime and every sort of social ill;
- deepening resentment on the part of Negroes, leading to acts of violence;
- growing resentment of that violence by whites.

[18]

Where will it lead? Where *can* it lead? There are bitter and violent people on both sides who hope for the worst. But the rest of us have to believe that a saner path is possible.

Hatred and violence used to be chiefly the stock in trade of the white racist. Then they became the stock in trade of the Negro extremist. But there is a curious contrast between the two. Negro hatred of whites is often expressed openly. It is frankly defended and widely discussed. In contrast, white hatred of Negroes has gone underground. It is rarely discussed publicly, rarely debated candidly. Indeed, when the President's Commission on Civil Disorders spoke of it openly, many people thought the authors of the report had done an unseemly thing.

Yet the white hatred is there. And everyone knows it. The long tradition of white brutality and mistreatment of the Negro has diminished but has not come to an end.

It still excludes Negroes from white neighborhoods and bars them from many job opportunities. No Negro reaches adulthood without having been through many experiences with whites that bruise his self-respect and diminish his confidence.

Such attitudes on the part of whites must come to an end if this nation is to survive as a free society. Each one who adds his bit to the storm of hatred does his share to move us toward a final reckoning that no free American will like.

Negro extremists who advocate violence assert that nonviolence did not work. It is untrue. The greatest gains for the American Negro came in response to the nonviolent campaigns of Martin Luther King and (before it turned violent) the Student Nonviolent Coordinating Committee.

It is the fashion now to belittle those gains, but they were great and undeniable. They were registered in historic civil rights legislation, and even more emphatically in social practice. Compare Negro voting patterns today with those prevailing as little as three years ago; or Southern school desegregation today with practices of four years ago; or patterns of restaurant and hotel desegregation over the same period or employment opportunities now and then.

The gains are not enough. They cannot satisfy our conscience. But they were great. And they came in response to nonviolence.

The violent tactics of the past two years have brought nothing but deepened hostility between the races and a slowing down of progress in the necessary drive toward social justice.

Many white liberals have now allied themselves with the Negro extremists in the sanctioning of violence. They speak approvingly of past riots as having "dramatized" the problem. They never speak of the negative consequences of the riots, but everyone who observed the session of Congress that followed the riots of 1967 knows that the negative reactions were a reality, and diminished the possibility of constructive solutions.

Nor do those who condone violence ever speak of the legacy of bitterness and division that will be left by increasingly harsh outbursts of destructive interaction. What good will it do to dramatize the problem if, in the process, hatreds burn themselves so deep that the wounds permanently cripple our society? Nor do those who condone violence ever face up to the likelihood that paroxysms of public disorder will lead ultimately to authoritarian countermeasures.

19

The comfortable American does not enjoy thinking about the human misery festering at the other end of town. He does not enjoy knowing that many of his fellow citizens live in conditions that breed every variety of social evil. It is not easy for him to acknowledge that his own infant, dropped into that ruinous environment, would just as surely fall victim to it. He averts his eyes from the human damage that occurs there.

In the absence of medical attention, physical deficiencies that could be corrected early become lifelong handicaps. In the absence of early mental stimulation, minds that could be awakened settle into lifelong dullness. Crime, drugs and prostitution claim their victims. So do apathy, degradation and despair. Ultimately all Americans bear the cost.

A disintegrating neighborhood and its social casualties are in every way a burden on the community and the nation.

Poverty is not easy to eliminate, whether the poor are black or white. In the case of the Negro it is made harder by the evil of racism.

But we cannot afford to be discouraged by the difficulty of the problems. If they were easy, we would have solved them long ago. When we formed this free society, we did not commit ourselves to solve only the easy ones.

We now recognize that poverty is deeply rooted—in the early deprivation of the child, in his parents' lack of education, in their feelings of resignation and apathy and defeat, in the slum environments that confirm such attitudes, and in the urban disorganization that permits and promotes a high rate of social casualties.

We have learned that when people have been subjected to extremes of social isolation or cultural poverty or deprivation of one kind or another, we must do more than just give them opportunities to learn. We must take positive steps to help them break out of the prison of self-doubt, apathy and fear.

As little as twenty years ago, most educators would have told you that all we need do with such people is to provide them with opportunities and those who are worth their salt will learn. We now know better. We know that these individuals need not only instruction but confidence, not only books but motivation. They need to be able to hope. They need to have some sense of their own worth. They need to believe in themselves.

All of these things we are now trying to learn how to provide.

The fate of the urban poor and the urban Negro is bound up with the fate of the city, and the city is in grave trouble.

Some of the city's troubles are physical—transportation, water and sewage, pollution, slum dwellings, lack of open space and so on. But the most menacing ills of the city are at bottom not physical but social. One could recite the familiar list of specific social ills—crime, poverty, segregation. But beneath and behind all of these we are faced with problems of social organization, of governance, of politics in the Aristotelian sense of the word.

In the past, those who have planned the physical renewal of our cities have given all too little thought to the social consequences of their bricks-and-mortar judgments.

And those concerned with social consequences have not been sufficiently aggressive in demanding a voice in decisions of this sort.

We need to reassess the adequacy of our social services in the poverty areas of cities. With all our efforts, federal, state and local, we are not providing enough service to enough people; we are not providing a high enough quality of service; the services we do provide are not always accessible to those who need them most; and existing services are frequently uncoordinated, with the result that they either hotly compete for or totally ignore whole groups of clients.

The plain fact is that most cities are not organized to cope with their problems. Their haphazard growth has brought such rampant administrative disorder that good government is scarcely possible.

The schools alone cannot solve the problems of poverty and segregation, particularly those schools already harnessed to the slums. They will never be fully effective against those problems until educational planning is linked to planning in land use, transportation, recreation, health care, social services and broad new patterns of metropolitan and school governance.

The Economic Opportunity Act of 1964 is remarkable if only for its rejection of the proposition that the ease of the well-to-do must rest on the discomfort of the poor.

ⁱ

In low-income areas roughly six out of every ten children who suffer from chronic health problems are not receiving any treatment.

Welfare payments are much too low in a good many states. That is a widely accepted fact among all who are concerned with these programs; indeed, it is probably the most widely agreed-upon fact among welfare experts today.

I do not believe that the federal government should continue to support programs in which needy people are expected to live on amounts which the states themselves say are not enough to maintain a minimum level of decency and health.

Many of the problems encountered by the welfare program will not be solved within the context of the welfare program itself. They are rooted in the fact of poverty and all that goes with it—bad housing, poor schools, dismal and decayed neighborhoods, crime, family life that is often unstable, and the feelings of despair, apathy and hopelessness harbored by so many who are trapped in such environments. Poverty itself is the enemy, and it will take a good deal more than changes in the welfare system to conquer it.

I do not believe that children should have to pay for the shortcomings and inequities of the society into which they are born. I do not believe that children should have to pay for the real or supposed sins of their parents. And I think it would be shortsighted of a society to produce, by its neglect, a group of future citizens very likely to be unproductive and characterized by bitterness and alienation.

Of all the ways in which society serves the individual, few are more meaningful than to provide him with a decent job.

We cannot have communities half sound and half unsound. Bitterness, anger and social disintegration cannot be sealed off. They will inevitably affect the whole community and the whole nation. It isn't going to be a decent society for any of us until it is for all of us. If our sense of responsibility fails us, our sheer self-interest should come to the rescue.

CHAPTER V

PROBLEM-SOLVING

For our generation there's no such thing as life without trouble. There are only good kinds of trouble and bad kinds of trouble.

The bad kind of trouble stems from apathy, stagnation, the kind of hypocrisy that refuses to admit the existence of problems, the kind of vested interest that prevents institutional change. The good kind of trouble comes from being on the move, from being acutely aware of problems, from the confusion of too many people trying to solve the problem in too many ways all at once, too many critics talking too loudly, too many things changing too rapidly.

A generation doesn't have much choice in the problems that the forces of history throw in its lap. It does have a choice as to whether it will face those problems honestly. We need continuous and candid debate as to what the most important problems are, and whether we're turning our backs on them or solving them or making them worse.

9

If we look at our present capacity to solve problems, it is apparent that we do best when the problems involve little or no social context. We're skilled in coping with problems with no human ingredient at all, as in the physical sciences. We are fairly good at problems that involve the social element to a limited degree, as in biomedical research. But we are poor at problem-solving that requires the revision of social structures, the renewal of institutions, the invention of new human arrangements.

Not only are problems in this realm exceedingly complex, but in some cases we are rather strongly motivated *not* to solve them. Solving them would endanger old, familiar ways of doing things.

We have learned brilliantly the means of accomplishing scientific and technical advance. But we have a very limited grasp of the art of changing human institutions to serve our purposes in a changing world.

The consequences are familiar. We can build gleaming spires in the hearts of our cities, but we can't redeem the ghettos.

We can keep people alive twenty-five years beyond retirement, but we can't ensure that they can live those years in dignity.

We choke in the air that we ourselves polluted. We live in fear of a thermonuclear climax for which we provided the ingredients. We face a population disaster made more probable by our own healing arts.

Social change is a learning process for all concerned. It

always requires re-education of large numbers of people to accept new objectives, new values, new procedures. It cannot go forward without the breaking down of long-established ways of doing and thinking. This is true whether the problem is one of civil rights, the reform of local government, educational improvement or urban renewal. Most human institutions are designed to resist such learning rather than facilitate it.

Some people seem to believe that for each problem there is a solution readily available—a solution that can be promptly achieved by passing a law and voting some money.

I think of this as the vending-machine concept of social change. Put a coin in the machine and out comes a piece of candy. If there is a social problem, pass a law and out comes a solution. When the nation fails to solve one of its problems promptly, people who hold such a simplified view naturally assume that someone in power was stupid or misguided or both.

I don't want to rule that out as a possibility. But the truth is that we face a number of extremely puzzling problems to which no one has the answers, problems that are nobody's fault.

Social change takes time. That is a sentence which no one pressing for change likes to utter. I don't like to utter it. It is the business of the proponent of social change to be impatient.

But we're caught in a dilemma. If we pretend that social change doesn't take time, we're back to the vending-machine concept. And the consequences are predictable: unrealistic optimism as the change is initiated, disillusionment when it fails to ripen instantly.

I talked recently with a college student who had worked in the slums for three months. He was discouraged because he couldn't see signs of change despite the fact that his dedication had burned with a gemlike flame for one whole summer. I think I persuaded him that another summer or two might be necessary.

This is the day of the iatrogenic illness, the illness caused by the medicine itself. Any government department, indeed any organization setting out to cure social ills, had better be sure it isn't creating problems as rapidly as it cures them.

We must all face the coming crunch between expectations and resources. The expectations of the American people for social benefits are virtually limitless.

The proponents of every social institution or group believe passionately that support of their field must be vastly enlarged in the near future. The colleges and universities have ideas for federal support that would run to billions per year. And they ask little compared to the advocates of aid to elementary and secondary education.

The annual cost of a guaranteed income would run to scores of billions. Estimates of the cost of adequate air- and water-pollution control and solid-waste disposal run even higher. Estimates of the cost of renovating our cities run to hundreds of billions.

How do you make rational choices between goals when resources are limited—and will always be limited relative to expectations? The question translates itself into several others: How can we gather the data, accomplish the evaluation and do the planning that will make rational choices possible?

One striking feature of our situation today is that we are creating new problems as we go along. Consider the problems posed by some of the new mind-affecting drugs. Consider the economic, ethical and social problems posed by the possibility of artificial organs, or weather control, or the control of genetic processes. Environmental pollution is the classic example of a problem arising from our progress.

Our capacity to create new problems as rapidly as we solve the old has implications for the kind of society we shall have to design. We shall need a society that is sufficiently honest and open-minded to recognize its problems, sufficiently creative to conceive new solutions, and sufficiently purposeful to put those solutions into effect. It should be, in short, a self-renewing society, ready to improvise solutions to problems it won't recognize until tomorrow.

Our society today is a very primitive problem-solver. It need not be so.

Life never was a series of easy victories (not even a series of hard victories). We can't win every round or arrive at a neat solution to every problem. But driving, creative effort to solve problems is the breath of life, for a civilization or an individual.

CHAPTER VI

PEOPLE AS PROBLEM-SEEKERS

M<small>Y FRIEND</small> Caryl Haskins, who is president of the Carnegie Institution of Washington, points out that scientists are "problem-seekers." Unlike most of the rest of mankind, who regard problems as something to be avoided, the scientist goes out and looks for them. If he cannot manage things so that his life is an endless succession of problems, he counts himself a failure.

It seems clear to me that this pattern leads to the optimum life for man. And the ordinary citizen is far better fitted for such a life than he realizes.

Most men throughout history have spent their lives desperately trying to solve problems they did *not* seek out, and failure to solve those problems has all too often meant trouble and tragedy. It is hardly surprising that men have come to think of happiness as the absence of problems.

ᵟ

Total absence of problems would be the beginning of death for a society or an individual. We aren't constructed to live in that kind of world. We are problem-solvers by nature —problem-seekers, problem-requirers.

This is so much the case that when the problems of the real world aren't pressing in upon us, we invent artificial problems, such as how to reduce our golf score.

Golfers and scientists have quite a lot in common. They both face problems of their own choosing. And they take frank delight in the never-ending *process* of trying to solve the problems they have chosen.

In my opinion, that's living.

Recreational games are, of course, the least exciting games. Walter Bagehot said, "Business is really more agreeable than pleasure; it interests the whole mind, the aggregate nature of man more continuously and more deeply. But it does not *look* as if it did."

He was right. And there are activities even more exciting than business, because they engage even *more* fully the intellectual resources and values and social motivations of man—science, teaching, governing. Those activities involve companionship, novelty, risk, chance-taking, skill, team play, competition and all the other attributes of diversion. And they mean something.

What could be more satisfying than to be engaged in work in which every capacity or talent one may have is needed, every lesson one may have learned is used, every value one cares about is furthered?

No wonder men and women who find themselves in that

situation commonly overwork, pass up vacations and neglect the less exciting games such as golf.

It is one of the amusing errors of human judgment that the world habitually feels sorry for overworked men and women—and doesn't feel a bit sorry for the men and women who live moving from one pleasure resort to the next. As a result, the hard workers get not only all the real fun but all the sympathy too, while the resort habitués scratch the dry soil of calculated diversion and get roundly criticized for it. It isn't fair.

Some will argue that a life of continuous problem-solving bears a depressing resemblance to the life of Sisyphus. In the legend, Sisyphus was condemned to push a great stone to the top of the mountain, and just as he reached the top it would slip from his grasp and roll to the bottom and he would have to push it up again—and so on for all eternity. But the late Charles Curtis pointed out that it was the monotony, not the futility, of the task that made it punishment. If he could have rolled a different stone each time, or the same stone up different mountains, or if he could have experimented with improved ways of rolling it, it might not have been so bad. Certainly, as Curtis pointed out, it would have been better than just loafing around Hades.

CHAPTER VII

THE SOPHISTICATED DROPOUT

IF YOU want to avoid the toughest problems facing your generation, there are some classic forms of escape.

One is to get so wrapped up in your personal life—job, family, bills, house repairs, bridge parties, office politics, neighborhood social competition and the like—that there just isn't time for the larger problems of the day.

A more subtle exit from the grimy problems of the day is to immerse yourself so deeply in a specialized professional field that the larger community virtually ceases to exist. This is a particularly good way out because the rewards of professional specialization are very great today, so you may become rich and famous while you are ignoring the nation's problems.

Still another and infinitely devious means of turning your back on the larger community is to assert that the whole society is so corrupt that nothing can save it. Such moral gamesmanship relieves the gamesman of all responsibility. With one shrug he shakes off the burden that serious men have carried from the beginning of time: the struggle to make an imperfect society work.

A variation on that theme is to tell yourself that the society has fallen into the hands of unworthy people, and that virtuous, clear-eyed spirits such as yourself haven't a chance. You can suck that lollipop of self-deceit all your life long and die secure in the belief that the world would have been different had they turned it over to you.

This is the day of the sophisticated dropout. It used to be that those who stood aside from the significant, larger concerns of the society were mainly people whose perspective had not been broadened by education or people who were too shallow to take any matter seriously. Now we have a whole new category of educated, intelligent people who find immensely sophisticated reasons for noncommitment.

One variety of sophisticated dropout—perhaps the variety that annoys me most—proceeds by declaring the society so corrupt or the Establishment so deaf that there's no use trying. He washes his hands of the whole social enterprise because he judges it to be morally beneath him. The tactic seems incredibly simple (or simply incredible), but it's the going thing.

For serious men, since the beginning of time, the world's blemishes defined their task. Now the blemishes are the excuse for dropping out.

This is true of left-wing nihilists. It is true of irrational extremists of the right. (Rejecting the requirements of rationality is a particularly popular way of dropping out at the moment.)

Their common trait is that their dissent is a form of self-indulgence. And it is not through self-indulgence that we will get on with the back-breaking work of building social change into resistant human institutions. If this imperfect society is to be bettered, it will require men whose commitment is unshaken by the confusion and moral ambiguities of the real world.

I have little sympathy with those who have impossibly high hopes for social betterment and then the next day are wallowing in disillusionment and self-pity because their high hopes weren't realized. Social change isn't that easy. Creating a better world isn't that easy. Life isn't that easy.

We are producing the most educated, articulate and brilliant sidewalk superintendents the world has ever seen. We have a limitless supply of people with the intelligence and expertise to analyze the society's problems, but very, very few with the motivation and stamina to leap in and help solve them.

The capacity to destroy through criticism has achieved an advanced state of development in some sectors of the press and in some of our more sophisticated journals. The mark of merit is to cut everyone down to size, to blame, to demolish those whose views aren't identical with one's own. You hack away at me and what I stand for, and I'll hack away at you. The result: a landscape littered with mutilated bodies and razed structures. Nothing admirable, nothing alive except the insatiable zest to destroy, dissect and demolish, nothing left standing except some outsized critical egos.

The rebellious individualists of the nineteenth century paved the way for an army of followers. By the time the century was finished, any young man intelligent enough and literate enough to know his own tradition could rebel in the grand manner. Today it doesn't even require intelligence or education. The opportunity for estrangement has been fully democratized.

Where growth and creativity are concerned, a certain buoyancy is absolutely essential. A mood of wise and weary disenchantment may seem wonderfully mature, but it does not account for much of the growth and movement and vital action in the world.

The young people of this generation are perhaps more alert to the problems of the larger society than any preceding generation has been. But as they move on into their careers it is all too likely that their concern will diminish. For all their activism, they show every indication of following the time-honored trend—a few years of indignant concern for social betterment, characterized by a demand for immediate solutions to all the world's problems, and then a trailing off into the apathy and disinterest of the young executive or professional.

Our intellectual upper class is a very privileged class indeed. Its adult members live well, travel the world, have access to the mass media, sell their advice and services for large sums. Youthful members are given generous scholarships and enjoy an unexampled mobility and freedom from responsibility.

It is distressing to see that privileged class drift toward the rocks on which every such class in history has gone aground: arrogance, contempt for other groups in the society, insensitivity to the rest of the community.

Today we see some of its young members riding roughshod over community sensibilities as arrogantly as young seventeenth-century aristocrats horsewhipping the peasants.

The oldest excuse in the world for moral aimlessness and corruptibility is the argument that "everybody's doing it." We still hear it every day. I hear it in the most astonishingly sophisticated forms. The misbehaving modern almost strangles with self-pity as he contemplates the rotten world that made him what he is. Perhaps it is best to let him strangle. He is confused, but it is a purposeful confusion, and he won't thank you for clearing it up.

Every example of moral excellence that we know anything about—and they are sufficiently numerous and varied to hearten any man—has occurred in an environment shot through with moral flaws. Indeed, that is the nature of the human environment. It is the seedbed of corruption as well as decency, of degradation as well as greatness, of malice as well as of love.

CHAPTER VIII

THE LIFE AND DEATH

OF INSTITUTIONS

Most human organizations that fall short of their goals do so not because of stupidity or faulty doctrines, but because of internal decay and rigidification. They grow stiff in the joints. They get in a rut. They go to seed.

We have all seen young organizations that are still going through the diseases of childhood. And we have all seen organizations so far gone in the rigidities of age that they ought to be pensioned off and sent to Florida to live out their days.

There is a pleasantly unpredictable quality about institutional vitality. One can't build a great institution—a great university, for example—as one would put together a prefabricated house: knowing the ingredients and simply arranging for their assembly at an appropriate time and place. Nor can one repair a second-rate or dispirited institution the way one might repair a leaky roof.

In the perspective of decades and centuries, institutional greatness is a transitory thing. The appearance of greatness is more enduring.

Reputation and tradition are effective cosmetics for the fading institution.

What is all too transitory is that fine moment when an institution is responding with vigor and relevance to the needs of its day, when its morale and vitality are high, when it holds itself to unsparing standards of performance.

Organizations go to seed when the people in them go to seed. And they awaken when the people awaken. The renewal of organizations and societies starts with people.

In recent years, most organizations have come to recognize that their continued vitality depends on aggressive recruitment of talent. But the still untapped source of human vitality, the unmined lode of talent, is in those people already recruited and thereafter neglected.

The quickest and most effective road to renewal of the federal service is the mining of that untapped resource. It is not only a means of tapping unused talent and opening up new stores of vitality; it is a solution to the old, old problem of developing a government service that is responsive to changing top leadership. Vital people, using their gifts to the full, are naturally responsive. People who have stopped growing, defeated people, people who no longer have confidence in the use of their own powers, build bastions of procedure between themselves and any vital leadership.

We like to think that institutions are shaped according to the best vision of the best men in them, and sometimes they are. Let me put that more positively: history offers many persuasive examples of just that consequence—able and vigorous men sharing a vision of how they might shape their future and creating institutions to that end. But that is not the only way that institutions get shaped. Sometimes they are simply the sum of the historical accidents that have happened to them. Like the sand dunes in the desert, they are shaped by influences but not by purposes. Like our sprawling and ugly metropolitan centers, they are the unintended consequences of millions of fragmented purposes.

At least in some measure men can shape their institutions to suit their purposes, provided that they are clear as to what those purposes are, and provided that they are not too gravely afflicted with the diseases of which institutions die— among them complacency, myopia, an unwillingness to choose, and an unwillingness on the part of individuals to lend themselves to any worthy common purpose.

When we talk about revitalizing a society, we tend to put exclusive emphasis on finding new ideas. But there is usually no shortage of new ideas; the problem is to get a hearing for them.

The body of custom, convention and "reputable" standards exercises such an oppressive effect on creative minds that new developments in a field often originate outside the area of respectable practice. The break with traditional art was not fostered within the academy. Jazz did not spring from the bosom of the respectable music world. The land-grant colleges, possibly the most impressive innovation in the history of American higher education, did not spring from the inner circle of higher education as it then existed. Motels, the most significant development of this generation in innkeeping, were at first regarded with scorn by reputable hotel people.

Professions are subject to the same deadening forces that afflict all other human institutions: an attachment to time-honored ways, reverence for established procedures, a pre-occupation with one's own vested interests, and an excessively narrow definition of what is relevant and important.

Self-congratulation should be taken in small doses. It is habit-forming, and most human institutions are far gone in addiction.

Most ailing organizations have developed a functional blindness to their own defects. They are not suffering because they can't *solve* their problems but because they won't *see* their problems. They can look straight at their faults and rationalize them as virtues or necessities.

I would lay it down as a basic principle of human organization that the individuals who hold the reins of power in any enterprise cannot trust themselves to be adequately self-critical. For those in power the danger of self-deception is very great, the danger of failing to see the problems or refusing to see them is ever-present. And the only protection is to create an atmosphere in which anyone can speak up.

The most enlightened top executives are well aware of this. But I don't need to tell those readers who are below the loftiest level of management that even with enlightened executives a certain amount of prudence is useful. The Turks have a proverb that says, "The man who tells the truth should have one foot in the stirrup."

Perhaps the most important characteristic of an ever-renewing system is that it has built-in provisions for vigorous criticism. It protects the dissenter and the nonconformist. It knows that from the ranks of the critics come not only cranks and troublemakers but saviors and innovators. And since the spirit that welcomes nonconformity is fragile, the ever-renewing society does not depend on that spirit alone. It devises explicit legal and constitutional arrangements to protect the critic.

Why be so considerate of dissent and criticism? To answer that question is to state one of the strongest tenets of our political philosophy. We do not expect organizations or societies to be above criticism, nor do we trust the men who run them to be adequately self-critical. We believe that even those aspects of a society that are healthy today may deteriorate tomorrow. We believe that power wielded justly today may be wielded corruptly tomorrow.

The traditionalist believes that foolishness frozen into custom is preferable to foolishness fresh off the vine. And in some respects he is right.

We are always corrupting the old symbols, drifting away from the old truths. Give us a clean, clear, fresh idea or ideal and we can guarantee, within one generation, to render it positively moldy. And I don't mean health-giving penicillin mold. I mean the strictly nontherapeutic, nonnutritive mold of habit, apathy, complacency and lip service. We smother our values in ritual and encrust them with social observances which rapidly become meaningless.

Most organizations have a structure that was designed to solve problems that no longer exist.

An organization must have some means of combating the process by which men become prisoners of their procedures. The rule book grows fatter as the ideas grow fewer. Almost every well-established organization is a coral reef of procedures that were laid down to achieve some long-forgotten objective.

As a society becomes more concerned with precedent and custom, it comes to care more about *how* things are done and less about *whether* they are done. The man who wins acclaim is not the one who "gets things done" but the one who has an ingrained knowledge of the rules and accepted practices. Whether he accomplishes anything is less important than whether he conducts himself in an "appropriate" manner.

There are plenty of old pros who use their skill and experience to block progress rather than advance it.

The phrase "vested interests" has been associated with individuals or organizations of wealth and power, but the vested interests of workers may be as strong as those of the top executives. In any society many established ways of doing things are held in place not by logic nor even by habit, but by the enormous restraining force of vested interests. In an organization certain things remain unchanged for the simple reason that changing them would jeopardize the rights, privileges and advantages of specific individuals—perhaps the president, perhaps the maintenance men.

The vast, leaden weight of vested interest is everywhere—in the building codes that block renewal of the construction industry, in the featherbedding rules of union contracts, in the departmental structure of our universities, in the military services, in the functioning of Congress. No one has ever found a sure way to combat such vested interests.

Whenever a reorganization is proposed, some people object because they have become inseparably attached to old arrangements. I advise against all such attachments. Put your faith in ideas, ideals, movements, goals. Don't put your faith in organizational forms. Human beings are forever building the church and killing the creed. They give such loving attention to organizational forms that the spirit is imprisoned.

Every society must for its own good celebrate the qualities it values most highly and ceremonially recognize the men and women who embody those qualities.

9

When a top executive is selecting his key associates, there are only two qualities for which he should be willing to pay almost any price—taste and judgment. Almost everything else can be bought by the yard.

Everyone wants the government to be bold and imaginative and infallible—all at the same time. It will never happen.

Is the federal government bureaucratic? It is, indeed! But so are business firms, universities, the military services, state and local governments and philanthropic organizations.

Is the federal government in danger of going to seed? It is in the gravest danger! But so are all other organizations, large and small.

There is no excuse for government to lose out in the competition for talent. It has a built-in advantage over every other employer. The cynics would deny this, but the truth is that talented people are attracted to government because it gives them an opportunity to render service to the entire nation. They come with the highest motives. They leave when their purpose is thwarted or when they begin to feel trapped. Government cannot afford to be inhospitable to such people.

One may argue, as Toynbee does, that a society needs challenge. It is true. But societies differ notably in their capacity to see the challenge that exists. No society has ever so mastered the environment and itself that no challenge remained, but a good many have gone to sleep because they failed to understand the challenge that was undeniably there.

CHAPTER IX

ON CHANGE

Nicholas murray butler used to insist that in the Garden of Eden Adam paused at one point to say, "Eve, we are living in a period of transition." It was true for Adam. It was true for Nicholas Murray Butler. And it is very much more true for us.

Is change "a good thing"? Not necessarily. The American optimism with respect to change has its excesses, among them the notion that change is inevitably beneficial and good for its own sake. The proposition is not easy to accept. Death is a form of change. So is deterioration.

No society can invite change for the sake of change. It must court the kinds of change that will enrich and strengthen it rather than the kinds that will fragment and destroy it.

There are old ways of doing things that must be discarded and old values that must be preserved.

9

If some kinds of change are bad, and some kinds good, how can we know one from the other? The answer is that much of the time we can't.

Since we cannot really know what kinds of changes will prove useful, we must experiment. Or to put it more realistically, those of us who are temperamentally fitted for it must experiment, and the rest of us must tolerate it, even encourage it.

A system that isn't innovating is a system that is dying. In the long run, the innovators are the ones who rescue all human ventures from death by decay. So value them. You don't have to be one yourself, but you should be a friend of the innovators around you. And if you don't have any around you, you had better import some.

If a man has a new idea, you can neutralize him by throwing him into jail or you can neutralize him by refusing to listen. We do plenty of the latter.

The word "creativity" has achieved a dizzying popularity. It is more than a word today, it is an incantation. It is a kind of psychic wonder drug, powerful and presumably painless, and everyone wants a prescription.

The support of creative people is not in the nature of a business arrangement. It is always a gamble. The creative individual cannot say what he is likely to accomplish.

Money won't induce creativity. You can't tempt people to it or drive them to it. Neither the carrot nor the stick is useful.

One doesn't necessarily have to think up imaginative programs to serve imaginative people. Some thoroughly routine kinds of programs may be of immense benefit to the creative man. Often he needs a good housekeeper more than anything else in the world.

From all that we know of the creative individual, he thrives on freedom. Recent research shows that he is not the capricious and disorderly spirit some romantics have imagined him to be. He may be quite conventional with respect to all the trivial customs and niceties of life. But in the area of his creative work he must be free to believe or doubt, agree or disagree. He must be free to ask unsettling questions and free to come up with disturbing answers.

When Alexander the Great visited Diogenes and asked whether he could do anything for the famed teacher, Diogenes replied, "Only stand out of my light." Perhaps someday we shall know how to heighten creativity. Until then, one of the best things we can do for creative men and women is to stand out of their light.

Today we can't afford not to take chances. I am always puzzled by people who talk as though the advocates of change are just inventing ways to disturb the peace in what would otherwise be a tranquil community. It would not otherwise be a tranquil community. We are not seeking change for the sheer fun of it. We must change to meet the challenge of altered circumstances. Change will occur whether we like it or not. It will be either change in a good and healthy direction or change in a bad and regrettable direction. There is no tranquillity for us.

We can choose not to accept the challenge, of course; but then we shall fall very rapidly into the ranks of the museum nations, and tourists from more vigorous lands will come from afar to marvel at our quaint ways.

I am less interested in inducing any particular change than I am in fostering and nourishing the conditions under which constructive change may occur.

CHAPTER X

HEALTH

Health has a great deal to do with the quality of our lives. It is both an end and a means in the quest for quality, desirable for its own sake, but also essential if people are to live creatively and constructively. Health frees the individual to live up to his potential.

We have said that the good life is possible not only for the favored few but for all the people. And we have said that each person should have the opportunity to fulfill the possibilities that are in him. That is why we seek to arrange things so that every American will enjoy the liberation and fulfillment that are possible through education. And that is why we should strive to make the blessings of health just as widely available.

There is growing awareness of the gap between our performance and our potential in health. The contrasts are startling, and made even sharper by the dazzling promise of our science and technology.

American medicine has extraordinary achievements to its credit, but its benefits are not available to all our people. Indeed, a good many are almost untouched by those benefits.

The revolutions—social, economic, scientific—which have so greatly enhanced and so greatly complicated our ability to provide health services require no cataloguing here. But I would emphasize their results: a vastly more sophisticated people; one taught, and rightly so, to seek the full benefits which progress has made possible; a people who live longer and are thus more vulnerable to disease and dependency in later life; a society in which the gap between what is possible for some and inaccessible to others has widened and deepened; a society in which our performance lags far behind our potential.

Those who are least able to cope with the system—the disadvantaged—are the very ones most in need of medical care.

The results show up starkly in our mortality statistics, particularly for Negroes in urban ghettos. Maternal and infant death rates have gone down in the United States, rapidly in the early parts of this century, relatively slowly in the past twenty years. But the differences between white and nonwhite groups have increased.

Maternal mortality among nonwhite mothers is now almost four times that for white mothers, and infant mortality is two to three times higher for nonwhite than for white infants. That is not because we don't know how to reduce infant mortality. It's because we haven't been able to make adequate information and care available.

Often, the only care available to the poor is fragmented, impersonal and of inferior quality. But the medical situation is almost as frustrating for those who are better off economically. Too often they are bounced from one specialist to another, with their identity getting lost in the shuffle. Rich and poor alike are inconvenienced by crowded waiting rooms. Rich and poor alike are threatened by shortages of people and equipment. And no one is happy about the steep rise in medical prices.

Consumers must have a greater voice in health affairs.

The existence of a potential benefit isn't enough if it never gets into the hands of those who need it. This applies to health services available to the middle-class part of town but not to the slums a few blocks or a few miles away. Services must be organized so that they reach everyone who can profit from them. Otherwise, "equality of opportunity" becomes an empty phrase.

Everyone seems to agree that the existing system—or lack of system—for the delivery of health care has serious shortcomings. But there is not yet any agreement as to what the perfect system would look like. It seems likely that we will go through a period of experimentation and in true American fashion end up with several variations in different parts of the country, suiting local preferences and conditions.

Most health services have developed in a chaotic fashion, unrelated to each other or to the reality of the need.

[54]

Some areas are rich in hospitals or clinics, but essential laboratory and supporting services may be nonexistent.

Little thought has been given to the homebound or to the patient who needs to move freely or frequently from the hospital to the convalescent home to his own home.

Community programs are focused on disease categories instead of on people.

The result is a fragmentation of services, an inefficient use of resources and, worst of all, inferior care for the individual. Our attention has been riveted on pieces of the puzzle—manpower, facilities and especially financing. The central issue of planning and organization was sidetracked for more than thirty years by the bitter debate which ended with the adoption of Medicare.

We can't avoid some alteration of the natural world we live in. But man, even industrial man, is a part of nature, and must find some limit to the headlong destruction and fouling of the natural environment. How much fouled air can we breathe? How much filth can we spew into our rivers and lakes without disastrous consequences? How much bleakness and ugliness can we tolerate around us?

We have begun to recognize that there are limits to our thoughtless use of the atmosphere as a sewer. Our concern is not merely with a suffocating haze that offends our senses, that soils laundry and buildings, that damages crops and corrodes metal. We are dealing with a killer. People become sick and they die from breathing dirty air.

Our choices are narrow. We can remain indoors and live like moles for an unspecified number of days each year. We can issue gas masks to a large segment of the population. We can live in domed cities. Or we can take action to stop fouling the air we breathe.

One way or another, this nation will bring the problem of air pollution under effective control. It will be done more quickly and more efficiently if industry contributes to the work in full measure. Efforts to find new and improved techniques for controlling air pollution must be given a priority which, until now, has been reserved for the development of new products and markets. It is industry, rather than government, that should take responsibility for carrying on most of the needed research and development. Those industries which make the greatest contributions to the nation's air-pollution problem have an obligation to make an equal contribution to its solution. They can afford to do so.

Cleaning up the air will call for a far greater investment of time, money and creativity than we have yet been willing to devote to it.

Some people keep hoping for a simple, quick or painless solution. It will never emerge. The technical, economic and social factors involved are immensely complex.

Air pollution, like other environmental problems of metropolitanism, is compounded of improper land use, choked transportation, poor disposal of waste and general lack of foresight in industrial and city planning. Controlling the sources of pollution might involve a community decision to invest in mass-transit facilities rather than in new highways. It might call for the dispersal of factories and plants that spill contaminants into the air. It might depend on the use of new types of fuel and new sources of power.

The air is only part of our total environment and pollution only one of the ravages that our civilization has wreaked upon it. We also have garbage dumps, dying lakes and poisoned rivers, noise, crowded communities, absence of green space, ugliness all around us. Surely this is not the net gain of our great technology nor the legacy we want to leave to other generations!

More and more Americans feel threatened by runaway technology, by large-scale organization, by overcrowding. More and more Americans are appalled by the ravages of industrial progress, by the defacement of nature, by man-made ugliness. If our society continues at its present rate to become less livable as it becomes more affluent, we promise all to end up in sumptuous misery.

Despite the overwhelming evidence, more Americans are smoking today than ever before.

The cigarette industry still maintains that the hazard of cigarette-smoking is an open question. This clouding of the issue may be contributing to the fact that cigarette consumption is almost back at the record level of 1963—4,345 cigarettes per year for every person eighteen and over.

We need to acknowledge the seriousness of the problem of smoking and health. It is irresponsible to hold out any comfort to cigarette smokers and potential smokers. There is a hazard.

For millions of Americans alcoholism is a cruel threat to

life, liberty and the pursuit of happiness. We have been slow to see it as such because we have been mesmerized by our deep moral disapproval of those who drink to excess. Socially we treat them as sinners. Legally we treat them as criminals. Medically we barely treat them at all.

Now we recognize that alcoholism is an illness and that our ways of dealing with this illness have been shockingly inadequate. (Even if it were not illness, even if it deserved no other name than folly, we should want to seek the means of correcting it. Folly is our common ailment.)

For our society, which has made such inroads on the traditional obstacles to individual fulfillment—tyranny, want and physical illness—there remains an unconquered giant. The greatest remaining enemy of human promise is the capacity of the human mind itself—and the emotions—to serve as an obstacle to effective functioning. The debilitating mental and emotional difficulties that plague "normal" people are the most powerful and universal constraint on human performance.

When we speak of enabling each individual to achieve his full promise, one doesn't think immediately of mental illness as a major obstacle. But in fact it is one of the worst. It strikes one out of ten Americans and fills nearly half of our hospital beds. It costs this nation billions of dollars each year. And its cost in terms of human woe must be seen to be comprehended. What it can do to a career, to the texture of family relationships or to an individual's confidence in himself can be harsh, even catastrophic.

No other health measure could more quickly and decisively diminish human misery, here and all over the globe, than the universal spread of family-planning information and services.

Every woman should be free to choose the number and spacing of her children. If she is too ignorant to know that the choice is available to her, she should be instructed. If she is too poor to afford family-planning services, they should be placed at her disposal.

There are those who say of the mentally retarded, "Why spend scarce resources of energy, talent and money on human beings who will never contribute significantly to the society, who will always be marginal?" I would give two answers, the first a practical answer and the second a conclusive one.

The practical answer is that the result of the effort is often the difference between a self-sufficient human being and one who is dependent, helpless, a burden to himself and society. We can achieve the former and avoid the latter for most retarded children.

The conclusive answer is much briefer: every individual is of value.

CHAPTER XI

QUALITY AND EQUALITY

IF WE ACCEPT the common usage of words, nothing can be more readily disproved than the old saw, "You can't keep a good man down." Most human societies have been beautifully organized to keep good men down.

We cannot have islands of excellence in a sea of slovenly indifference to standards. Today the masses of people are neither mute nor powerless. As consumers, as voters, as the source of public opinion, they heavily influence levels of taste and performance. They can create a climate supremely inimical to standards of any sort.

If the man in the street says, "Those fellows at the top have to be good, but I'm just an ordinary mug and can act like one," then the future of our society is very dim indeed.

That is why we need a broad conception of standards embracing many kinds of excellence at many levels. This is the only conception of excellence that fully accords with the richly varied potentialities of mankind, and it is the only one that will permit large numbers of Americans to strive for and achieve excellence in forms accessible to them—in craftsmanship, in personal integrity, in the discharge of parental duties and so on. To the extent that large numbers of Americans have sought for and achieved excellence at their own level of functioning, they will honor excellence at more complex levels of functioning.

On the one hand democracy is the form of society which rewards winners regardless of origin. On the other hand it is the form of society which gives losers the widest latitude in rewriting the rules of the contest. No one who has not thought long and hard about these paradoxical facts is in a position to understand the tug of war between equality and excellence in a democracy. When the rewriting of the rules is prompted by the standards of fair play, by elementary considerations of justice, by basic value judgments as to what sort of a "best man" the society wants, democracy can have no quarrel with it. Indeed, it is the core process of a democracy. But when the rewriting of the rules is designed to banish excellence, to rule out distinguished attainment, to inhibit spirited individuals, then all who pray for the continued vitality of democracy must protest.

Every democracy *must* encourage high individual performance. If it does not, then it closes itself off from the mainsprings of its dynamism and talent and imagination, and the traditional democratic invitation to the individual to realize his full potentialities becomes meaningless. Because of the leveling influences which are inevitable in popular government, a democracy must, more than any other form of government, maintain what Ralph Barton Perry has called

[61]

"an express insistence upon quality and distinction." When it does not do so, the consequences are all too familiar: the deterioration of standards, the debasement of taste, shoddy education, vulgar art, cheap politics and the tyranny of the lowest common denominator.

Those in a democracy who are most seriously concerned to foster excellence and the full realization of individual potentialities must be the first to comprehend the problem facing society as a whole. A society which accepts performance as the chief determinant of status—as ours does—has great charm for those whose ability, drive, aggressiveness or luck enables them to come out on top. It may have notably less charm for those who do not come out on top. These latter may be individuals of lesser ability or lower motivation. Or they may be individuals whose excellences do not add up to the sort of performance that society at any given moment chooses to reward. Or they may simply lack a temperament that takes kindly to the knife edge of competition. There are many individuals of great gifts in the latter group.

At any rate, for whatever reason, there are large numbers of individuals who will not necessarily find unrelieved exhilaration in a system that emphasizes high performance. If these large numbers come to believe that the system exposes them unnecessarily to frustration and defeat, and if they enjoy the freedom of social action characteristic of a democracy, they will create elaborate institutional defenses against the emphasis on performance. We can observe such institutional defenses not only in education but in every aspect of our national life.

19

This is not the place to explore the innumerable invitations to mediocrity which exist in our kind of society. Suffice it to say that they do exist and that their very existence requires powerful counterpressures. Free men must cherish what Whitehead has called "the habitual vision of greatness." Those of us who are most deeply devoted to a democratic society must be precisely the ones who insist upon excellence, who insist that free men are capable of the highest standards of performance, who insist that a free society can be a great society in the richest sense of that phrase. The idea for which this nation stands will not survive if the highest goal that free men can set themselves is an amiable mediocrity.

In some matters we as a people seem unstintingly committed to recognize excellence, to cherish high standards of quality, and, in the words of William James, "to disesteem what is cheap, trashy and impermanent." But on other fronts we exhibit more than a little inclination to enshrine the mediocre, to fear and scorn the superior performance, and to tie down every Gulliver who appears.

One of the requirements of social effectiveness in many segments of our national life is that one not arouse envy through an unseemly display of intelligence or talent. One must be, above all, unthreatening to the other fellow's self-esteem. In this atmosphere it will surprise no one to learn that deliberately slovenly speech, the studied fumble and the calculated inelegance have achieved the status of minor art forms. And the phrase "I'm just a country boy" has become the favored gambit of sophisticated and wily men.

Keeping a free society free—and vital and strong—is no job for the half-educated and the slovenly. In a society of free men competence is a primary duty. The man who does his job well tones up the whole society. And the man who does a slovenly job—whether he is a janitor or a judge, a surgeon or a technician—lowers the tone of the society. So do the chiselers of high and low degree, the sleight-of-hand artists who know how to gain an advantage without honest work.

Some critics note that we discriminate nicely between excellence and mediocrity in athletics but refuse to be similarly precise about differences in intelligence; and they attribute this to the fact that we are more seriously concerned with athletic ability than with intelligence. Nothing could be further from the truth. We can afford, emotionally speaking, to be candid and coldly objective in judgments of athletic ability precisely because we do not take these as total judgments on the individual and as necessarily central to his self-esteem.

The reason we are reluctant to label individual differences in native capacity is that native capacity holds a uniquely important place in our scheme of things. In a stratified society, performance is not an important factor in establishing the individual's status, so he can afford to be less deeply concerned about his native capacity. For every step that a society takes away from a system of traditionally determined status toward a system in which performance is the chief determinant of status, the individual will be increasingly concerned about his native gifts.

The educational world has gone through phases of intensive concern for the gifted, for the average student and for the slow learner. But our kind of society demands the maximum development of individual potentialities *at every level of ability.* Today we are trying to repair our neglect of the slow learner. But it will serve no purpose to replace our neglect of the slow learner with a neglect of all others. We are all too prone to such wild swings of the pendulum in our national life. Martin Luther said that humanity was like a drunken peasant who is always ready to fall from his horse on one side or the other, and in that respect we Americans are all too human. We must learn to see the achievements and shortcomings of our educational system in some sort of embracing perspective which will permit us to repair one omission without creating others.

The good society is not one that ignores individual differences but one that deals with them wisely and humanely.

If we are really serious about equality of opportunity, we should be infinitely serious about individual differences, because what constitutes opportunity for one man is a stone wall for the next man. Individuals differ vastly from one another, and they differ in innumerable ways. If we are to do justice to the individual, we must seek the kind of education that will open *his* eyes, stimulate *his* mind and unlock *his* potentialities. There is no formula for this, and it may or

[65]

may not involve what we now think of as a college education.

The never-ending talent hunt, the incessant testing programs and the emphasis upon achievement will create a heightened awareness of individual differences at much earlier age levels. One can hardly regard this as a wholly attractive consequence. Indeed, it is in some respects highly unattractive. One must hope that ways will be found to soften the edge of competition and minimize harsh comparisons of individuals. And one must hope, too, that we shall have the wisdom to avoid a tyranny of the aptitude tester.

Some people may have greatness thrust upon them. Very few have excellence thrust upon them. They achieve it. They do not achieve it unwittingly, by "doin' what comes naturally"; and they don't stumble into it in the course of amusing themselves. All excellence involves discipline and tenacity of purpose.

There may be excellence or shoddiness in every line of human endeavor. We must learn to honor excellence (indeed, to *demand* it) in every socially accepted human activity, however humble the activity, and to scorn shoddiness, however exalted the activity. An excellent plumber is infinitely more admirable than an incompetent philosopher. The society which scorns excellence in plumbing because plumbing is a humble activity and tolerates shoddiness in philosophy because it is an exalted activity will have neither good plumbing nor good philosophy. Neither its pipes nor its theories will hold water.

CHAPTER XII

EDUCATION

W<small>E ALL KNOW</small> in our bones that over the long haul what we do in education has the greatest relevance to building the kind of society we want.

America promises that everyone shall have a chance to achieve his full potential, and education is the chief instrument for making good that promise. It is the path to individual fulfillment. Our aim is to make it an avenue broad enough for all to travel.

The history of American education is the long, turbulent record of a nation that wasn't afraid to risk failure or trouble or confusion in pursuit of a goal that at first seemed wildly impractical: to give every American child a chance to develop to the limit of his ability. It is still one of the most radical ideas in human history, yet it grew out of the American soil as naturally as wheat or corn.

6

You cannot understand the educational system in the United States unless you understand that it is the indispensable instrument of the revolution in human social organization which has taken place on this continent over the past two centuries.

The effort to educate all our citizens entails certain consequences. It means mass education. It means crowded schools and huge universities. It means devising educational programs for youngsters who will grow up to be plumbers and farmers as well as for those who will grow up to be philosophers and art critics. In short, it is a very different system from one designed to educate young aristocrats for the role of cultivated gentlemen. We have set ourselves a task of astonishing dimensions. And having set ourselves these objectives, we cannot weep because our educational system no longer resembles the cozy, tidy world we deliberately put behind us.

Much education today is monumentally ineffective. All too often we are giving young people cut flowers when we should be teaching them to grow their own plants. We are stuffing their heads with the products of earlier innovation rather than teaching them how to innovate. We think of the mind as a storehouse to be filled rather than as an instrument to be used.

In the United States, college professors who look at secondary education with a critical eye almost invariably start from the mistaken assumption that the highest function of the secondary school is to prepare youngsters for college.

That isn't true. The first purposes of American education are to foster individual fulfillment in all children and to nurture the free, rational, responsible men and women without whom our kind of society cannot endure.

Ultimately, education serves all our purposes—liberty, justice and all our other aims—but the one it serves most directly is equality of opportunity.

We wish the individual to fulfill his potentialities, but obviously we do not wish to develop great criminals or great rascals. We wish to foster fulfillment within the framework of rational and moral strivings which have characterized man at his best. In a world of huge organizations and vast social forces that dwarf and threaten the individual, we must range ourselves whenever possible on the side of individuality; but we cannot applaud an irresponsible, amoral or wholly self-gratifying individuality.

Educational policy is shaped, after all, whether or not men give serious thought to it. It is determined by economic factors, by popular demand, by national need, by the pressures of the market, by parents and students, and by the moods and fads of the moment. It is determined by the men who set tuition levels, by the men who formulate admissions policies, by alumni who want a better football team, by psychologists who devise entrance examinations, by employers who demand certain kinds of training, by professional associations seeking to advance their fields, by givers of money, by pressure groups.

I am entirely certain that twenty years from now we will look back at education as it is practiced in most schools today and wonder that we could have tolerated anything so primitive.

The pieces of the educational revolution are lying around unassembled.

The great strategy with young people is to keep their development sufficiently broad so that when they become mature enough to make a choice, it may be a choice among many significant possibilities.

As an institutional system American education is not tightly knit. At its best it is loosely knit, at its worst completely unraveled. It's a mystery that it works at all. But that's how we want it and that's how it is going to remain.

Although we have in effect a nationwide educational system, it is by no means a centralized one. The local school district is the main point of decision and initiative in the system. But at least part of the time we have to think of our educational efforts in nationwide terms. Not only are we engaged in a common effort, but all the various parts of our educational system are interrelated and affect one another.

The unemployment rolls of St. Louis, Detroit and Chicago include men and women who were inadequately educated in the schools of Alabama and Mississippi. When Northeastern states fail to provide enough tax-supported higher education for their high school graduates, those young people crowd into public institutions from Ohio to Oregon. When a scientist in Cambridge, Massachusetts, develops a new physics curriculum, it affects every high school in the nation.

Education needs more than dollars. It needs to be better than it is—not just somewhat better but a great deal better. We are not going to succeed in making it that much better, nor succeed in solving the major problems facing us, without substantial innovation. Without such innovation new billions poured into the system will simply strengthen and confirm outworn practices.

All the organizational arrangements, all the methods and procedures that characterize American education today were originally devised to help us accomplish our purposes. If they no longer help us, we must revise them. The arrangements and methods must serve us and not control us.

If you ask seven mathematics teachers about the new math, you'll get seven different answers. You don't need to be an expert on set theory to know that that's a lot of disagreement. And many educators are unhappy about it. But the moral is simply that it isn't the function of innovation to make you happy.

Anyone in the field of teacher education today who is not impatient with the status quo and eagerly seeking new solutions is more insulated from reality than he has any right to be.

Love of learning, curiosity, self-discipline, intellectual honesty, the capacity to think clearly—these and all the other consequences of a good education cannot be insured by skillful administrative devices. The quality of the teacher is the key to good education.

Some subjects are more important than others. Reading is the most important of all.

From the earliest years girls should be actively encouraged in the development of their intellectual capacities. Teachers, guidance people and parents should recognize that women are capable of advanced education in any field, including mathematics, science, engineering, medicine and law.

Women should be encouraged to enter every field requiring advanced training. A woman's family obligations may make it necessary to modify the pattern of graduate and professional training established by and for men. Her professional career may also involve departures from the masculine norm. Colleges and graduate schools should make it easy for women to continue their education part time (or to interrupt it) during the period of heaviest family obligations.

Our thinking about the aims of education has too often been shallow, constricted and lacking in reach or perspective. Our educational purposes must be seen in the broader framework of our convictions concerning the worth of the individual and the importance of individual fulfillment. It is now time to insist that this larger framework be universally explored and understood.

In a sense this is an obligation we owe to those great shapers of the Western tradition who taught us the importance of individual fulfillment. They gave us the blueprints for a cathedral, but a good deal of the time we insist on referring to it as a toolshed.

All education worthy of the name enhances the individual. It heightens awareness, or deepens understanding, or enlarges one's powers, or introduces one to new modes of appreciation and enjoyment. It promotes individual fulfillment. It is a means of self-discovery.

We can never understand the profound American commitment to education if we concentrate on one or another of its specialized consequences—employability, cultural literacy, enjoyment of leisure and so on. In the deepest sense, we are committed to education because it enables one to live more fully in the dimensions that are distinctively human.

It has been fashionable to blame educators for every shortcoming of our schools, but educators cannot maintain standards of excellence in a community that cares more about a marching band and a winning basketball team than it does about teachers' salaries.

The final justification of all the billion-dollar programs, all the lofty educational policy, all the organizational efforts is that somewhere an individual child learns something that he might not have learned, or grows in understanding, or gains in skill or capacity or insight.

I am proud of the scope and reach of our educational objectives today. If we come anywhere near achieving them, we will transform the society.

[73]

CHAPTER XIII

SCHOOLS AND SOCIETY

IN THE SLUMS of our great cities today boys and girls who could easily be brought to the full use of their powers are left stunted, inarticulate and angry.

Considering our tradition of local control, it is surprising to find that the schools have been in some respects quite insulated from the surrounding community.

Because the American school was not actively concerned with the rest of the community, it paid little attention to the problems of poverty and discrimination. It was slow to recognize the importance of early childhood education and slow to see the importance of working with disadvantaged parents as well as disadvantaged children.

When students were troublesome or backward, the school simply unloaded them on the community and forgot about them.

The result is that the community—often with federal help

—proceeded to develop a whole array of out-of-school programs for dropouts. Americans are an impatient people. If they have important purposes that are not served by existing institutions, they invent new institutions. When the public schools did not appear to be meeting the growing concern about poverty, new programs were invented, many outside the school system.

This is an understandable reaction. But if the trend continues, we will end up with two school systems—one for middle-class youngsters who attend the conventional schools and one for disadvantaged youngsters. Such a division of the school population by social and economic class is not the kind of system we started out to build in this country, nor is it the kind of system we want.

The schools could be the seedbeds of a new America, free of racial injustice. Instead, all too often they confirm old attitudes and ways.

Are the schools organized and administered in such a way as to exemplify the best that the society can do to advance racial understanding? The answer, I'm sorry to say, is no. The schools could be a major ingredient in the solution— instead, they're a part of the problem.

What are we teaching about civil rights in the schools? Practically nothing. Is it not surprising that our children learn little or nothing in school about the most divisive and agonizing problem in American life? Is it not possible that if they understood the roots and reasons for the great struggle we are engaged in today, they would be better prepared to work out a just and enduring solution?

Segregated schools, North and South, fail to give their students the critically important experience of knowing and working with members of another race. If professional educators who bear the responsibility for creating good schools fail to insist on desegregation, fail even to plead its cause in the community, who will do it for them?

We are now beginning to understand that when we are trying to teach people who have for many years been subordinated or excluded or discriminated against or in other ways made to doubt their own value, we must first of all repair the damage to their own sense of worth. This is true whether we are dealing with former colonials in Africa or field workers in Venezuela or Navahos in our own Southwest or Negroes in Alabama.

I have been giving some attention to the education of American-Indian children, Mexican-American children, Puerto Rican children in New York City, Negro children North and South, and to education in the developing nations. I now believe that there is a profound similarity in the educational problems of all children who have been kept out of the mainstream of modern culture by social or economic circumstances. If we can learn how to cope with such problems, we will have broken a sonic barrier with a report that will echo and reverberate in every underdeveloped nation in the world.

❂

Fatalism is an all-smothering obstacle to purposeful effort and therefore to learning and therefore to any significant self-improvement.

Learning occurs when people have some measure of confidence and hope.

CHAPTER XIV

LAYMEN AND THE SCHOOLS

LAYMEN bear the ultimate responsibility for education in our society. They are the school board members. They serve on the state boards of education. They are trustees of colleges and universities. The President and Congress are laymen, not professional educators. And so are most voters.

There must be priorities in education as in any other field of social endeavor. And it is up to laymen to make the final decisions on those priorities.

But the laymen who carry such heavy responsibilities for American education are mostly volunteers. And the tradition of voluntary activity in this country involves a charming combination of goodwill and inefficiency, enthusiasm and casualness, zest and lack of follow-through.

Today the lay interest in education is fragmented into tens of thousands of organizations, communities, councils—no one of them with adequate resources to have significant impact on the behemoth of American education.

Give some thought to how lay concern for education is organized.

Do we have adequate arrangements so that the interested layman can get an independent appraisal of what's going on in American education?

Do we have the machinery for independent lay opinion to make itself felt?

Frankly, I don't think so.

I believe that nongovernmental and nonprofessional sources should be monitoring educational developments continuously—identifying the crucial issues, providing independent appraisals of those issues, and disseminating the results as widely as possible.

We are not now organized to accomplish that.

School people may find themselves longing for the good old days when nobody paid attention to them. But criticism and second-guessing by the layman are at least in part a positive mark of public interest, and the price of public support. The taxpayer is justified in asking us to remember the ancient proverb, "If you would have a hen lay, you must bear with her cackling."

Every community needs to ask these questions:

- Does it have first-rate people on its school board, and are they broadly representative of the community?
- Does the board have open lines of communication to the

school administration, to the teachers and to the entire community?

- Is it getting the information it needs to make responsible decisions, both short- and long-range?
- Does it have effective liaison with allied community programs: with the departments of health and welfare, with housing, private industry, transportation and total city planning?
- Is it doing what a board should do—setting the policy for a strong administrator responsible to it—or is it wasting its time by dabbling in administrative details?

If you get an affirmative answer to all these questions, you're likely to have a first-rate public school system. If not, then your work is cut out for you.

Most school boards in this country are inadequately organized to do their job. I have known hundreds of able and experienced men and women who suffered years of service on a badly organized board, but only two or three who tried to reduce the frustrations through a reorganization of the board.

The way education is organized often determines its effectiveness, so critics of the system must sooner or later come to grips with it.

The plain truth is that many of the states have not yet developed strong, effective and well-staffed departments of education and are not yet equipped to provide the kind of leadership in education that our society needs today.

Big-city school people are apt to be extremely skeptical of any move that would strengthen educational machinery in the state capital. Many of them believe that they have been treated shabbily by the state capital in the past. They consider that the most attractive feature of state educational machinery today is that it is too weak to do them much harm.

Weak it certainly is. But it is folly to imagine that such weakness is a virtue. The state has a role that *cannot* be played by the local district and *must not* be played by the federal government. If it isn't strong enough to play that role well, it will play it badly. If it cannot contribute to progress, it can often block progress.

In the American educational pattern federal, state and local leadership must *all* be vigorous and effective. No one of the three should assume that it will be stronger if the other two are incompetent.

CHAPTER XV

REFLECTION AND ACTION

THE LIFE of reflection is not superior to the life of action nor vice versa. Both are essential to a vital society.

The serious gulf between the career of action and the career of reflection must be narrowed. The universities, as they prepare some young men for lives of scholarship and others for lives of action, must be conscious of the problem. In this era of complexity, great enterprises are designed and carried forward by the kind of man who has a vision of what might be *and* a practical strategy for getting there, a man with an idea in his head and a monkey wrench in his hand.

Each individual has to decide how much he wants to become personally involved in the action and effort of his society. There is no correct answer. The individual must decide in terms of his own temperament and motivation.

A society that aspires to creativity has urgent need of its detached scholars and critics, as well as of those who will become deeply involved in the world of action.

Creativity requires the freedom to consider "unthinkable" alternatives, to doubt the worth of cherished practices.

Every organization, every society, is under the spell of assumptions so familiar that they are never questioned—least of all by those most intimately involved.

There is a certain perspective on any social enterprise that can be had only from the outside. That is why De Tocqueville was able to see our country as no American of the time could see it. That is why corporation presidents seek the advice of outside management consultants. That is why anthropologists can be objective about other cultures but not about their own.

People at the heart of an enterprise are striving with all their energy to accomplish certain objectives. They haven't time to doubt and speculate, and even if they did, it would be a risky form of self-indulgence.

That is why it is so essential that there be people who have the time and the detachment to think not of the moment but of the past and the future, not only of how to solve the problem but whether it's worth solving, not only of what is but what might be.

But no society can survive, certainly not our own complex and swiftly changing society, if it fails to persuade a high proportion of its young people to choose the path of complete involvement in the actions and decisions of their day. We are in desperate need of talented and highly motivated young men and women to move into the key leadership and managerial roles in government, industry, the professions and elsewhere throughout the society.

Our society must have the wisdom to reflect *and* the fortitude to act. It must provide the creative soil for new ideas *and* the skill and patience and hardihood to put those ideas into action.

Philosopher-kings there never have been and never will be, except in the Platonic imagination. And yet every man who thinks seriously and consecutively about the problems of society finds himself groping toward some reconciling of action and reflection. My view is that though this will never happen, we can come as close to it as reality allows by maintaining good communication and open highways between the citadels of power and the citadels of reflection.

CHAPTER XVI

THE UNIVERSITIES:

IN AND ABOVE THE BATTLE

Universities don't spring up in the desert nor in primitive societies. A great university is the product of a great cultural tradition and a vital civilization. It can flourish only in a society that has the will to nurture such a tradition and the vitality to support it. It will not flourish if the civilization that supports it decays.

In short, universities have a stake in the health of their society.

There is in the academic world a tradition that the university must be somewhat separate from society. Certain kinds of scholarly and scientific activities have benefited considerably by that separation. At least a part of the university must *always* be a haven from the pressures of the society—a haven for dissent, debate, reflection and creative thought.

But from the beginning of our national life some leaders of thought have envisaged American universities as being intimately tied to the goals and strivings of the whole society, and as serving the society in very direct ways.

That was the view of Thomas Jefferson. It was the view of Benjamin Rush. It was a view that did not come fully into its own until the land-grant college movement. Alfred North Whitehead expressed the prevailing American view when he said, "Celibacy does not suit a university. It must mate itself with action."

Today the seemingly antagonistic traditions of separateness and involvement exist side by side in our greatest universities. At the heart of any great American university there is the kind of insulation from the market place that permits reflective and creative thought. At the same time, in other parts of the university, there is extensive interaction with the rest of the society.

I would not wish anything to alter the character of the university as a haven for dissent and for creative, scholarly work. That must be preserved at all costs. But I believe that those parts of the university which are already involved with the larger community are going to have to take that relationship more seriously than ever before. Some academic people —including close friends of mine—are advocating precisely the opposite position: less rather than more involvement. I respect their motives; I see the point of their arguments; and it grieves me that they should be so wrong.

The university community today is not indifferent to the agonies of the larger society. Almost all academic people are aware and concerned observers of the nation. Some are active technical advisers and sources of ideas for the larger community.

All are willing critics—but, for the most part, critics in the nonparticipant tradition of the husband visiting a millinery shop with his wife: "I like it," "I don't like it."

In adopting such a role the university is limited to re-acting to the alternatives that time and circumstance place before it.

That is not enough. We need in the university community a focused, systematic, responsible, even aggressive concern for the manner in which the society is evolving—a concern for its values, for the problems it faces, and for the strategies appropriate to clarify those values and to solve those problems.

We need men who are seeking new solutions and helping us on toward those solutions. We need designers of the future. We need to be told how to build a better society, and how to get from here to there. Most of all we need help in the difficult business of changing institutions.

When one moves from the scientific and technical arena to those problems involving change in human institutions, one cannot say that the universities are today a significant intellectual base for the main attack. In fact, a good many university people whose fields give them a legitimate interest in these matters barely understand what the relevant problems are. Many are debating policy alternatives that were left behind five years ago. Few are planning the kind of research that would sharpen policy alternatives.

Consider our most grievous domestic problems—the cluster of interlocking problems centering around poverty, the cities and the Negro. One would like to think that the universities have been the primary source of intellectual stimulation and enlightenment on these issues. One would like to think that university research on these matters had laid the basis for significant action. One would like to think that university people had played a key role in formulating the public policy alternatives, and in suggesting the factual or value considerations involved in each alternative.

Unfortunately, this is far from the truth.

I do not say that the universities should function in the world of action in a way that is indistinguishable from other institutions. It is not appropriate for a university to engage in propaganda. It is not proper for a university to engage in political maneuvering.

Everything that the university does in the world outside should be marked by its commitment to the highest standards of performance, its habit of taking the long perspective, its preoccupation with root problems, its intellectual approach to practical matters, its disciplined habit of mind, its commitment to the highest values of our culture, and its relative disengagement from the self-interested considerations which move protagonists in the day-to-day strife of the world.

In other words, in everything that the universities undertake they should be true to themselves. Only in that way can they exercise their great intellectual and moral influence to accomplish objectives within their own tradition.

Some academic people believe that the practical demands which society places on the university are not a blessing but a snare. They would rather be let alone, and their sentiment is well summed up in a Latin-American saying, *"No quiero el queso sino salir de la ratonera,"* which means "I don't want the cheese, I just want to get out of the trap."

There are those in the population, even among the alumni and on the boards of trustees of some universities, who resent the fact that the university is a haven for dissent and for the free examination of assumptions and practices. They often strive to diminish this fundamental role of a university. They seem to imagine that the chief role of the university is to endorse the status quo.

On the other side, there are some within the university community who seem to want to cut all ties with the rest of the society, and to persuade every last student to choose the life of detachment and dissent. They don't like the way the society is run, but they aren't inclined to prepare young people to run it better. And they communicate to their students a moral snobbism toward those who live with the ethical dilemmas of responsible action.

I hope that in preparing young men and women for lives as scholars and critics our universities will make them aware of the dangers in such irresponsibility.

I hope that in preparing them for the world of business and government the universities will make them appreciative of the social function of the scholar, the dissenter and the critic.

Finally, I hope the universities persuade a reasonable proportion of their graduates to move back and forth between the two worlds.

I like to think that no matter how much the university becomes entangled with the world on its outer fringes, the inner city of the university will be above the battle in some quite distinctive ways. I should like to believe that it will, to borrow some lines from Bernard Shaw, "stand for the future and the past, for the posterity that has no vote and the tradition that never had any . . . for the great abstractions, for the eternal against the expedient; for the evolutionary appetite against the day's gluttony; for intellectual integrity, for humanity, for the rescue of industry from commercialism and of science from professionalism." I like to think that it will stand for things that are forgotten in the heat of battle, for values that get pushed aside in the rough-and-tumble of everyday living, for the goals we ought to be thinking about and never do, for the facts we don't like to face and the questions we lack the courage to ask.

CHAPTER XVII

THE UNIVERSITIES:

MEANS AND ENDS

In 1937 one of my professors at the University of California said, "Throughout human history brains have been a drug on the market." Several years later a nationally known educator warned that the nation was overproducing bright, highly educated people and that there wouldn't be enough jobs for them.

Such views sound quaint today. Our society has become so complex, so dependent on specialization, that it cannot function effectively without a plentiful supply of educated talent.

The old-fashioned respect for higher education was based on the notion that it was really quite a nice thing if you could afford it, and if you had time for it, and if the society could afford it. It wasn't essential but was highly ornamental and most becoming to a gentleman.

A more modern view recognizes that the nature of our

society and our era has forced education, particularly higher education, into a central position in the society.

It cannot be said too often that more college degrees may not necessarily bring any increment in virtue or wisdom. Whether we shall have a steady flow into our leadership ranks of wise, liberally educated men and women with the creativity and sense of values the future demands or a paralyzing flow of skilled opportunists, timeservers and educated fools depends wholly upon the sense of values that guides our efforts.

College and university people are inclined to believe that the American public has not always rendered them an unsullied devotion. That is quite true; and a very good thing it is. The feeling that the American public is not as appreciative as it might be is not unique to academic people; it is shared by politicians, bankers, industrialists, generals, farmers, labor leaders and all professional entertainers, including big-league baseball managers. Of all of these, the colleges and universities probably have least cause for complaint. Indeed, if higher education in America deteriorates, it may very well be because the public loved it too well rather than too little.

It used to be said that the only cure for seasickness was to sit in the shade of an old brick church in the country. Similarly, it might be said that the only sure cure for our present educational troubles would be to withdraw entirely from the tumultuous and troublesome business of educating everyone to the limit of his capacity. But to do that would be to reject all that we believe in.

There is the danger that the universities, in their eagerness to please everyone, satisfy all demands, serve all needs and run off in all directions, will forget that their first job is to produce educated men and women, educated in the broadest and deepest sense of that word. There is more than a little hazard that we shall—with enormous zest and organizational skill—shuffle millions of students through utterly meaningless experiences and believe that we have accomplished something.

A college education comes to the student packaged in courses that he is supposed to sample systematically. And the student, pressed for time and caught in the routine of studies, works his way through the forest of courses like an industrious beaver chomping his way through the river saplings.

If one looks at student unrest around the country and attempts to sift the real issues from the extraordinary clutter of emotion and recrimination, it becomes clear that the students have hit upon at least one or two issues that go to the heart of the problem of the modern university. The question of whether undergraduate teaching is being neglected is a real one, and I am proud to say that in many colleges and universities the students have a genuine grievance. The question of anonymity and impersonality of student life is also a real issue in many institutions, a problem worthy of all our wisdom and inventiveness.

(9

All good education is both liberal and practical, and only the pedant tries to force them into separate categories.

There are two ways of thinking about a liberal education: one has to do with subject matter—with those fields of knowledge which are concerned with man's experience; the other has to do with teaching methods—with those methods which liberate and temper the mind. When we speak of a liberal education we should mean both things: the fields of knowledge which are the treasury of man's experience and the methods of teaching which liven and liberate his mind. No student in American higher education should miss either of these experiences, no matter what college he attends.

Liberally educated people will have sensed man's little-ness as well as his occasional greatness, his capacity to endure as well as his capacity to aspire, his infidelity as well as his faith and his faithfulness. Understanding these things, they will distinguish between the enduring excellences and the glittering prizes of the moment.

Until very recently the university as a community knew a good deal more about the mistresses of Louis XIV than it did about the American high school. But events of recent years have taught us that the welfare of higher education is inseparably linked to the quality and vigor of the elementary and secondary schools.

I have been surprised by the censorious tone with which some critics now refer to large universities, almost as though in growing to their present size these institutions had deliberately chosen to do an evil thing. This is ridiculous. The critics may, if they wish, attack the American people for holding such a liberal view concerning who should go to college. But they should not attack institutions that are simply trying to accomplish a well-nigh impossible task that the society has handed them. The institutions being scolded for largeness today are the ones that have been most responsive to the American eagerness to broaden educational opportunities. We should have the grace to live with the consequences of our choices.

There are incompetents in every line, and some achieve professorial rank.

Young people who go to college away from home encounter one particularly effective stimulus to personal growth: they find that there is no longer anyone to stand between them and the consequences of their own foolishness. It's a bracing experience.

One way to discover what are considered to be the important professions is to ask which professional schools receive highest priority in university planning. It is a rare campus on which the school of education is ranked first. Yet in terms of our national future, teaching is the most important profession.

The greatest American educational invention of the nineteenth century was the land-grant college. The greatest

American educational invention of the twentieth century is the two-year community college.

Any college, anywhere, that says it doesn't need more money is putting on airs. And I haven't run into many with that failing.

College presidents and deans live in an atmosphere of more or less continuous heckling, and unexpected praise can seriously disconcert them.

The university president has an extraordinarily difficult job. The press demands access to him, donors require courtesies, the general public expects pontifical statements. If he is not firm enough, the trustees will scold him; if he's too firm, the faculty will go up in smoke. If he's a father figure, all the students will love him except those who hate him. Among all the university president's varied constituencies, only we alumni are uncritical, docile, supportive and wholly lovable.

Little wonder that, under such grinding and debilitating pressures, most college presidents give up the hope of being educational leaders and settle down to the grim but necessary job of being custodians.

Faculty mobility may be excessive today, but too much of it is better than too little of it. It helps to keep institutions young, though it may make presidents old before their time.

Almost any proposal for major innovation in the universities today runs head on into the opposition of powerful vested interests. And the problem is compounded by the fact that all of us who have grown up in the academic world are skilled in identifying our vested interests with the Good, the True, and the Beautiful, so that an attack on them is by definition subversive.

The irony of our present situation is that the academics, despite themselves, have discovered the joys of organization. The scholar may say that he despises organization, but he quite complacently accepts—even demands—the benefits which it brings. When the far-flung and intricately organized money-raising operation of his university brings in enough dollars to raise his salary, he offers no resistance— not even nonviolent resistance. When his work in experimental biology leads him into research that can only be done with *Macaca rhesus* monkeys, he does not set out to catch them himself. He submits a request through channels, and the marvels of modern organization provide him with the monkeys in no time at all. And the delightful thing is that all the while these things are occurring, he is keeping up a running fire of criticism of the evils of modern organization.

Like every other social institution, universities are subject to disintegrative forces, are the scene of power politics, and are susceptible to the decay that so often sets in at precisely the hour of triumph.

I have noticed in the recent campus troubles that "administrator" has become something of a dirty word—the only

[97]

one not spelled with four letters and the only one that no one has risen to defend.

Nowhere can the operation of vested interests be more clearly seen than in the functioning of university departments. The average department holds on like grim death to its piece of intellectual terrain. It teaches its neophytes a jealous devotion to the boundaries of the field. It assesses the significance of intellectual questions by the extent to which they can be answered without going outside the sacred territory. Such vested interests effectively block most efforts to reform undergraduate instruction.

I don't like to see universities torn by dissension among students, faculty, administration and trustees. In this swiftly changing society, academic institutions are going to have difficulty surviving as coherent communities, and the difficulty will be magnified if they are expending their best energies in civil war.

The community that enjoys internal coherence and morale is in a position to defend and preserve its autonomy and to shape its future. The noncommunity will be shaped to a greater degree by outside forces.

Even if the campus loses every trace of community, it can still be a very busy, productive, important place—in the sense that a city block in the heart of one of our great metropolises is a busy, productive, important place. The fact that a group of activities are not welded into a community does not necessarily diminish their significance.

But it is hard to view that prospect with enthusiasm. The young people who pass through these institutions can profit immensely from membership in a local community that has its proud traditions and standards and *esprit*. Later they may shift their loyalty to nationwide or world-wide professional communities, but for the education of youth the face-to-face community has incomparable advantages.

The schools and colleges must equip the student for a never-ending process of learning; they must gird his mind and spirit for the constant reshaping and re-examination of himself. They cannot content themselves with the time-honored process of stuffing students like sausages or even the possibly more acceptable process of training them like seals.

CHAPTER XVIII

THE UNIVERSITIES

AND GOVERNMENT

Wʜᴇɴ government agencies and universities work together, there are predictable sources of difficulty. Surely we know those difficulties by heart now. I shall mention only two or three of the most salient problems.

The government agency tends to surround the relationship with more and more defining conditions, to the point where the university feels that its freedom of decision is undermined. This does not reflect a sinister desire to diminish anyone's freedom. It stems from the nature of government responsibilities and habits of mind. The remarkable thing is not that all agencies show these tendencies, which they do, but that some agencies have had the wisdom to curb them.

Just as the government agency tends to tighten the defining conditions of the relationship, so university people seek to loosen them. They tend to push all contracts and grants in the direction of the general support grant: fewer conditions, more freedom to define objectives and greater continuity of support. The ideal relationship as far as the university man is concerned would be one entirely without any complicating context, which is to say without any context at all, money passed in the dead of night from a donor who would never know the object of his largess to a recipient who would never know who gave the money or why. Some government observers refer to this as the "leave it on a stump" approach.

The attitude of the universities toward federal money reminds me a bit of the small boy who wrote home after his first week in boarding school, "Dear Mom: The food here is absolute poison—and such small portions!"

Universities bring to the government-university relationship a sense of intellectual and moral superiority that is extremely irritating when conflicts of purpose arise. The irritation is heightened by the fact that the university representatives are usually more articulate than those of government.

Professors tend to manifest the sense of moral superiority more aggravatingly than do deans or presidents. A faculty friend of mine says, "Naturally! They have more to feel superior about!" He didn't intend it as a joke.

As we all know, there exists among many faculty people (and, indeed, among professional men everywhere) a widely accepted myth concerning the purity of the professional and the corruptness of the administrator. On the one side, the myth asserts, there are scholars and professionals— pure and selfless spirits who think only of the high requirements of their calling; and on the other side, there are the administrators, organization men and politicians—seekers of power and status who achieve their aims by a willingness to compromise their convictions. The myth is sustained by frequent repetition of Lord Acton's aphorism. It is hardly surprising that these attitudes nourish a certain paranoia in the academic man who holds them: in every encounter with decision-makers he sees himself as the potential victim.

Yet the available evidence indicates that he is immensely skillful in advancing his own interests.

I would assert this as a general principle: In their dealings with government agencies the universities should worry almost as much about the health and competence of the agencies with which they are dealing as they do about their own autonomy. The relationship cannot be a healthy one if the government agency involved is weak, poorly staffed or disorganized. The evils flowing from that condition will impair the whole relationship.

Many of our present federally supported higher education programs contain legislated categories which are too narrowly defined to allow colleges and universities to derive maximum benefit from them. Moreover, the specific nature of some federal-aid categories often operates subtly to redirect and reorient the programs of a college or university in directions which are inconsistent with the institution's purposes.

It is clear that in dealing with the world of action, in dealing for example with the federal government, the universities must be highly selective. They have not been so in the past. A tremendous array of activities has been allowed to develop without an adequate guiding philosophy. When a government agency with money to spend approaches a university, it can usually purchase almost any service it wants. And many institutions still follow the odd practice of listing funds so received as gifts. They not only do not look a gift horse in the mouth; they don't even pause to note whether it is a horse or a boa constrictor.

As long as the universities have no conception of themselves other than the supermarket conception, they will have to resign themselves to the fact that people will walk in off the street, buy a box of Wheaties, and walk out.

As the university's involvement with the federal government moves from trivial to substantial, the administration has no choice but to ask with increasing rigor the following kinds of questions:

- Is the proposed activity compatible with the aims of the university?
- Where does it stand on a list of university priorities?
- Does it impair (or strengthen) the university's capacity to carry out its central mission?
- Is it something that a university is uniquely fitted to do, something that only a university can do?
- Will it result in growth or strengthening for the university itself?

We would be better off today if university administrations had asked these questions about a number of activities now in progress.

When I say that we must have greater understanding between government agencies and universities, I do not mean that the relationship should be more intimate than it is. Actually, it is in the public interest to keep a certain adversary quality in the relationship. Under such conditions, the agency is continually alert to the requirements of its mission, its accountability to the taxpayer and its constitutional responsibility. And the university never forgets that it was born free and should remain so, never forgets that its purposes are not identical with (indeed, sometimes at odds with) the purposes of the government agency. Neither of the participants loses its keen sense of separate missions and separate identities.

The issue of university autonomy will never be finally solved. It can only be lived with.

CHAPTER XIX

LEARNING THROUGHOUT LIFE

MANY whom the world counts as unsuccessful have
continued learning and growing throughout their lives, and
some of our most prominent people stopped learning literally
decades ago.

Perhaps the greatest challenge in education—and the
most puzzling one—is to discover what it is that keeps alive
in some people the natural spark of curiosity, eagerness,
hunger for life and experience, and how we may rekindle
that spark when it flickers out. If we ever solve that problem,
we will be at the threshold of a new era, not only in education but in human experience.

To sensible men, every day is a day of reckoning.

Commencement speakers are fond of saying that education is a lifelong process. And yet that is something that no
young person with a grain of sense needs to be told. Why do

the speakers go on saying it? It isn't simply that they love sentiments that are well worn with reverent handling (though that is undeniable). It isn't that they underestimate their audience. The truth is that they know something their young listeners do not know—and unfortunately something that can never be fully communicated. No matter how firm an intellectual grasp the young person may have on the idea that education is a lifelong process, he can never know it with the poignancy, with the deeply etched clarity, with the overtones of satisfaction and regret that an older person knows it. The young person has not yet made enough mistakes that cannot be repaired. He has not yet passed enough forks in the road that cannot be retraced.

It is not easy to tell young people how unpurposefully we learn, how life tosses us head over heels into our most vivid learning experiences, how intensely we resist many of the increments in our own growth.

Unfortunately, our institutional arrangements for lifelong education are ridiculously inadequate. Most educational institutions are still designed for young people who have nothing else to do. They are ill-suited to men and women who must fit their learning into a busy life.

Educational activities outside the schools and colleges enjoy little prestige and have had virtually no connection with the formal system. The educational world, after all, has its own snobbery. The dukes and earls of the graduate schools find it sufficiently burdensome to have to associate with the solid yeomen of the business school faculty, without having to tolerate the barefoot knaves who operate outside the formal system altogether.

The conception of individual fulfillment and lifelong learning finds no adequate reflection in our social institutions. For too long we have paid pious lip service to the idea and trifled with it in practice. Like those who confine their religion to Sunday and forget it the rest of the week, we have segregated the idea of individual fulfillment into one compartment of our national life and neglected it elsewhere. If we believe what we profess concerning the worth of the individual, then the idea of individual fulfillment within a framework of moral purpose must become our deepest concern, our national preoccupation, our passion, our obsession.

Aside from our formal educational system there is little evidence of any such preoccupation. Some religious groups are doing good work. Our libraries and museums are a source of pride. Adult education programs have become increasingly effective.

But what about moving pictures, radio and television, with their great possibilities for contributing to the growth of the individual? It would be fair to say that these possibilities have not dominated the imagination of the men who control these media. On the contrary, these media have all too often permitted the triumph of cupidity over every educational value. What about newspapers and magazines, with their obvious potentialities for furthering the intellectual and moral growth of the individual? At best a small fraction of the publishers accept such a responsibility. Book publishers, too, are not without fault.

Serious pursuit of the goal of individual fulfillment will carry us even further afield. Unions, lodges, professional organizations and social clubs can all contribute importantly to individual growth and learning if they are so inclined. Only sporadically have they been so inclined. There are innumerable opportunities open to the employer who is willing to acknowledge his responsibility for furthering the individual development of men and women in his employ.

The process of learning throughout life is by no means continuous and by no means universal. If it were, age and wisdom would be perfectly correlated, and there would be no such thing as an old fool—a proposition sharply at odds with common experience.

One of the reasons mature people stop learning is that they become less and less willing to risk failure.

If we live long enough, all of us are students and all of us are teachers. Every employer and every supervisor and every foreman is a teacher—perhaps a good teacher, perhaps a bad or neglectful teacher.

One of the happiest outcomes of an era that makes learning universal and lifelong will be a drastic scaling down of the emphasis on academic credits as a form of "payment" for learning. Anyone familiar with the wide variations in course content, teaching levels and grading practices knows that those payments are made in very uncertain currency, yet we cling to it as though it were pure gold. Taking the academic world as a whole, there are plenty of wooden nickels in circulation, but everyone is much too polite to say so.

Once we accept the idea of lifelong learning, much of the present anxiety over young people who quit school prematurely will disappear. The anxiety stems from the fact that today leaving school signifies the end of education. Under the new system there will be no end to education.

The more we allow the impression to get abroad that only the college man or woman is worthy of respect in our society, the more we contribute to a fatal confusion which works to the injury of all concerned. If we permit the faulty assumption that college is the sole cradle of human dignity, need we be surprised that every citizen demands to be rocked in that cradle?

The crowding in our colleges is less regrettable than the confusion in our values. Human dignity and worth should be assessed only in terms of those qualities of mind and spirit that are within the reach of every human being.

Being a college graduate involves qualities of mind that can never be universally possessed. Everyone does not have a "right" to be a college graduate, any more than everyone has a right to run a four-minute mile. The brain surgeon must have a level of intelligence that is rare in the population, and must subject himself to roughly twice as much schooling as the average man. That is not a question of rights. It is just a fact of life.

It is not the goal of a democracy that every citizen be the equivalent of a brain surgeon or a top executive. It is the goal of a democracy that every individual fulfill his own potentialities and live a meaningful and satisfying life in the context of those potentialities. The important thing is that he have the kinds of experience and education that will bring out the best that is in him. College will do that for some kinds of people with some kinds of abilities. Other kinds of experience will do it for people with different abilities.

The false emphasis we place on continued formal schooling has two unfortunate consequences. On the one hand, it exerts pressure on the young person to continue his schooling whether or not he has any taste or aptitude for it. This is often harmful to him; it is always costly to society; and it leads to make-believe education. On the other hand, if he drops out of high school or doesn't go to college, he is led to believe that he has landed on the scrap heap and that further learning or growth is out of the question. This is disastrous for his morale and in the long run dangerous to society. He is caught between alternatives both of which are an affront to his self-respect and neither of which seems to offer an honest promise of self-development. Do we really need to subject him to such indignities? I refuse to believe it. We cannot do anything immediately to alter the fierce overemphasis on continued formal schooling. But we might, if we act resolutely, devise a system that will avoid some of the worst evils that have flowed from that overemphasis.

Those who have been most sympathetic to the needs of academically less able children have tended to offer only one solution: more schooling. Sometimes more schooling is the answer, but there comes a time when it is not. And the failure to see constructive alternatives is leading us into deeper and deeper absurdities. It is leading too many of our young people into educational paths that gain them nothing except the conviction that they are misfits. The truth is that in the case of the youngster who is not very talented academically, continuance of formal schooling may simply prolong a situation in which he is doomed to failure.

We must not make the insolent and degrading assumption that youngsters unfitted for the conventional colleges are incapable of rigorous attention to *some sort* of standards. One of the most appalling and unhappy errors of much popular education has been to assume that youngsters incapable of the highest standards of intellectual excellence are incapable of any standards whatsoever and can properly be subjected to shoddy, slovenly and trashy educational fare.

While many high schools do a reasonably good—sometimes a very good—job in educating those young people whose abilities fit them for skilled work, very few do a good job with the boys and girls whose abilities do not come up to that standard. The average high school really doesn't know what to do with such boys and girls. For the most part it simply bears with them until school-leaving age and then turns them out into the streets.

Once the young person has left school, no one is officially concerned with his educational or vocational future. It is not usually regarded as a responsibility of the school. But it should be. We should not simply turn these boys and girls out on the streets. They need advice. They need jobs. They need to be helped to think constructively about their own abilities and limitations, about job opportunities and about their further learning and growth.

Bright youngsters are not directed to a library and told to get their own education; they are given guidance. Similarly, the young people who go out into the world after high school—and even more urgently those who drop out before graduation from high school—should be helped in order to assure that the years immediately ahead will be years of continued self-development.

To be specific, every high school in the land should provide *continuing* vocational and educational counseling for all who leave school short of college. These services should be available until the boy or girl reaches the age of twenty-one.

CHAPTER XX

THE PURSUIT OF MEANING

T HE RETIRED EXECUTIVE plunges into the lazy, diverting activities he always dreamed about, and within a year he is perfectly miserable. He itches for some meaningful work to occupy his mind and talents. What do you suppose is the matter with him?

I have a wide acquaintance among the leading scholars and scientists of this country, and most of them work at least a sixty-hour week, not because they have to and not with a sense of oppression, but with exhilaration. What can they be thinking of?

The conventional notions of happiness cannot possibly be taken seriously by anyone whose intellectual or moral development has progressed beyond that of a three-week-old puppy.

The reason Americans have not trapped the bluebird of happiness, despite the most frantic efforts the world has ever seen, is that happiness as total gratification is not a state to which man can aspire.

The irony is that we should have brought such unprecedented dynamism to the search for such a static condition.

The storybook idea of happiness tells of desires fulfilled; the truer version involves striving toward meaningful goals. Storybook happiness involves a bland idleness; the truer conception involves seeking and purposeful effort. Storybook happiness involves every form of pleasant thumb-twiddling; true happiness involves the full use of one's powers and talents. Both conceptions of happiness involve love, but the storybook version puts great emphasis on being loved, and the truer version more emphasis on the capacity to give love.

The more mature and meaningful view opens up the possibility that a man might even achieve happiness in striving to meet his moral responsibilities, an outcome that is unlikely under the present view, unless his moral responsibilities happen to be uncommonly diverting.

Each of us seeks, in Kierkegaard's vivid phrase, "a truth that is true for me." The present age is the first one in which large segments of the population have imagined that man might do without such a highly personal sense of the meaning of his life.

And for a breath-taking moment, it did seem possible, in view of the glittering promises with which modern life offered to distract man's attention. Science was to cure his ills. The new technologies would conquer the physical environment for him. The new political philosophies would dissolve the social hierarchy and make every man a king. The destruction of old and unnecessarily rigid moralities would give him a healthier and freer life of the senses. In short, he would have security, opportunity, money, power, sensual gratification, and status as high as any man. He would be a solvent and eupeptic Walter Mitty in a rich and meaningless world.

Comfort isn't enough. Ingenious diversions aren't enough. "Having enough of everything" isn't enough. If it were, the large number of Americans who have been able to indulge their whims on a scale unprecedented in history would be deliriously happy. They would be telling one another of their unparalleled serenity and bliss instead of trading tranquilizer prescriptions.

I don't want to be misunderstood. I don't want to be put down as an enemy of the pleasant things in life. You will not hear me telling poor people that they should be content with poverty or hungry people that hunger is ennobling. I would like every human being to have the chance to enjoy the comforts and pleasures of good living. All I am saying is that they are not enough.

We need a sense of identity, enduring emotional ties to others, a vision of what is worth striving for. Most of all we need a system of values that we consider worthy of our allegiance (even if it is subject to revision).

To be needed is one of the richest forms of moral and spiritual nourishment, and not to be needed is one of the most severe forms of psychic deprivation. There is danger in a conviction on the part of young people that they are not needed by their own community.

"The sense of uselessness," said Thomas Huxley, "is the severest shock which our system can sustain." The society which allows its young men and women to fall into this attitude is not simply neglecting them; it is depriving them of a powerful spiritual tonic. The truth is that we do need our young people, and we need them desperately. Instead of scolding them for their lack of purposefulness, our national leaders might devote a little more imagination to telling them why they are needed. Why not tell them that we've got hold of a man-sized job and need help?

The young people of our society have given ample evidence of their desire to create a better world.

Many of our best young people today wonder whether they have any place in this vast and complicated society of ours. They feel anonymous and rootless and alienated. They are oppressed by the impersonality of our institutions. In my judgment there isn't any quicker cure for that ailment than evidence that their society needs them. I don't think there could be anything better for a great many of our young people than a period of hard voluntary service in a venture surrounded by a spirit of dedication.

We must design new means for the individual to render service to the community, to the nation and to mankind. When President Kennedy said, "Ask not what your country can do for you; ask what you can do for your country," the response was great, but people didn't know quite what to do about it. The only new opportunity for service offered at that time was the Peace Corps, and its success was immediate. Later VISTA was created and has proven increasingly valuable. The Teacher Corps met with an enthusiastic response from young people. At the same time, service programs have been blossoming on college campuses.

When we set out to act in the service of our beliefs, we are capable of doing foolish things as well as wise things. Every mode of behavior has its pathology, and dedication is no exception. There are forms of dedication that we must regard as extremely unwise. A man may be committed to worthy goals but pursue them so fanatically as to destroy either his health, his family life or even the welfare of others in the community. And there is the "true believer" so well described by Eric Hoffer—a person who submerges himself in a cause because he wants to escape the responsibilities of life as an autonomous individual. We have a responsibility to commit ourselves to the things we believe in, but we have an even deeper obligation to play our role as free, rational and responsible individuals.

I do not recommend dedication as such, without regard to the goal. I'm sure the skill involved in pocket-picking requires dedicated effort, but I do not commend it.

One of the problems you encounter in talking about dedication is that everyone wants the other fellow to be more dedicated.

Some people strengthen the society just by being the kind of people they are.

*

The word "moral" is a lofty abstraction, but when we use it we are talking ultimately about behavior. The word cannot have any meaning without this final anchoring in behavior. If you want to do something to make the world better, start where you live. Start with yourself. Do a better job. Be a better friend. Live a better life.

I'm inclined to be down-to-earth in judging virtue. When a man says he loves mankind, I want to know how he gets along with his wife and his neighbors. When a man says he loves democracy and hates tyranny, I want to know how he treats his children and his subordinates.

Men of integrity, by their very existence, rekindle the belief that as a people we can live above the level of moral squalor. We need that belief; a cynical community is a corrupt community.

CHAPTER XXI

THE JUDGING MIND

It is in the modern mode for us to shrink from making judgments, even to believe that it is somehow presumptuous or arrogant to make judgments. We feel that it is more seemly to devise a system and let the system make the judgments, or invent a machine and let the machine do the judging, or gather statistics and let the statistics make the judgments.

Moderns are particularly reluctant to make moral judgments. Some have defended this reluctance by asserting that the neutrality with respect to values that is useful in certain kinds of scientific investigation is equally justifiable in everyday life. Others have waved the banner of moral relativity, pointing out—quite accurately—that our own moral precepts have shifted with the years, and that other societies have other moral precepts. Social scientists have achieved this perspective at the cost of great struggle, and we need not begrudge them the benefits. But when it is taken as a guide to daily living, it leads to a sort of moral *laissez faire*—

a notion that one must tolerate all sorts of values because after all we have no scientific proof that one value is better than another.

Some believe that such tolerance will somehow lead to a good result. In this view it is not necessary—or perhaps even seemly—to take sides in a moral controversy, because somehow the competition among values will work the whole thing out. In fact, one does not even need to believe in any particular values; one simply looks on from the sidelines with an amiable anthropological curiosity.

What interests me about moral neutralism or moral *laissez faire* is the illusion—a typically modern illusion—that the mind can abdicate its judging role.

Even those people who have argued most strongly that they must be neutral with respect to moral values have failed to live by that stern code. They continue to be morally indignant when someone cheats them. Statistics showing that a substantial proportion of the population are cheaters do not ease the indignation.

Some grammarians now tell us that we must not seek to judge good or bad usage in language but should accept existing patterns of usage, whatever they may be. I am not going to argue the point. I just want to call your attention to the recurrence of something not unlike a Kinsey approach: If enough people do it, it's all right. Look to the statistics! Pass no judgments! "Whatever is, is right."

The creative person has a richer and more varied array of ideas, images and hunches than the normal person. When he is trying to solve a problem, he has more hypotheses and more *varied* hypotheses. He is more open to experience, so that perceptions, images and possibilities flood in on him from outside. He is less rigidly resistant to ideas rising from the unconscious mind. At this stage of the creative process the watchword would appear to be "Anything goes!"

But there is a stage of the creative process that has received far less attention. The creative individual, who has opened himself up to such a rich and varied range of experience, exhibits an extraordinary capacity to find the order that underlies that varied experience, I would even say an extraordinary capacity to *impose* order on experience. All great creative performances involve precisely such an ordering of experience. And, indeed, it is possible that the creative individual would not be able to tolerate such a wild disorder of ideas and experiences if he did not have profound confidence in his capacity to find or impose some kind of pattern on this chaos.

It is interesting to ask why we have glorified the relatively undisciplined, chaotic phase of the creative process and almost ignored the disciplined, law-seeking, form-imposing side of creativity. The answer, at least in part, is that there is something about that aspect of the creative mind that doesn't quite suit the modern temper—something perhaps a little frightening. It is not a mind that seeks a consensus before it moves. The gifted artist may be humble before the stern requirements of his task, but when he is functioning at the height of his powers he trusts himself. The scientist of great originality may be humble before the natural order, but in the critical moments of creativity he has an almost breath-taking confidence in the capacity of his own mind to penetrate and comprehend some aspect of that order. In such moments both artist and scientist are more than a little imperious.

We fear the judging mind. Even more, we fear the judging and purposeful mind. And let's face the fact that we have reason to fear it. All of recorded history tells us what tyranny and dogmatism can flow from that mind. A good deal of social organization is designed to protect us from that tyranny. From the earliest times legal systems were at least in part a system of procedures that minimized the capricious judgment of any one individual. That is what we mean when we speak of a government of laws, not of men. Our own society is rich in social and organizational arrangements that protect the individual from being at the mercy of some other man's dogma and tyranny.

It would be catastrophic if we were to forget this distilled wisdom of the race. Yet the paradoxical truth is that the same judging, purposeful mind that can cause us such trouble is an important instrument of creativity and change and the source of all form and style.

The mind is an instrument of soaring possibilities and sordid limitations. It has the capacity to doubt and to believe, to reach out to the galaxies and to deceive itself about the simplest things, to conceive the highest ethical standard and to plot the most evil deed. It is capable of grandeur and of folly.

We cannot evade the necessity and the responsibility for using the mind to make judgments. It is not a matter of choice. "Life is fired at us point-blank," as Ortega y Gasset said, and there is really, literally, no place to hide. I was discussing these matters with a young man recently and he said, "I don't mind making judgments that involve myself alone, but I object to making judgments that affect the lives of other people." I sympathized, but had to tell him that his reluctance would make it impossible for him to be a second-grade teacher, a corporation president, a husband, a politician, a parent, a traffic policeman, a weatherman, a chef, a doctor or a horse-race handicapper—in fact, it would force him to live a hermit's life.

We may be reluctant to make moral judgments, but if we ignore that necessity it simply means that we shall make such judgments without being conscious of them.

We may be reluctant to make aesthetic judgments, but even the casual observer of our lives, our homes, our manner of expression will see that in fact we have made many such judgments—well or badly.

We may feel inadequate to the task of making political judgments, but the decision not to make political judgments is a decision with political consequences. So we have not really stayed out of that battle.

In short, we must use our minds to judge. We must use them as life requires, not just where we believe that judging is a sound and safe process but wherever life demands that we judge.

The tasks of parenthood alone force us into countless judgments that we are not ready for, judgments that we doubt anyone can make wisely. And so it is with the rest of life. It is filled with hazardous judgments. We make them consciously or unconsciously. We make them well or badly. But we make them.

It's the mark of a mature and thoughtful man that he sees this necessity. He not only sees the necessity, he sees the dangers. And he not only sees the dangers but he sees that some of them can be averted.

How may they be averted? First of all, by accepting the principle that every judgment is no more than a tentative approximation of the truth, subject to revision. In the phrase "subject to revision" we find the key to a modern role for the judging mind. If we recognize our judgments as subject to possible revision, we shall be less inclined to force them down other people's throats or to back them with bullets.

The other major principle in averting the dangers of human judgment lies in the training of the mind. The mind has an enormous capacity for error, self-deception, illogic, sloppiness, confusion and silliness. All these tendencies may be diminished by training, and that, of course, is the function of education.

CHAPTER XXII

LEADERSHIP

I HAVE a certain skepticism about the indiscriminate use of the word "leader." I always remember the wife who read the fortunetelling card her husband got from a penny weighing machine. "You are a leader," she read, "with a magnetic personality and strong character—intelligent, witty and attractive to the opposite sex." Then she turned the card over and added, "It has your weight wrong, too."

I have seen solemn descriptions of the qualities needed for leadership without any reference at all to the fact that the necessary attributes depend on the kind of leadership one is talking about. Even in a single field there may be different kinds of leadership which require different attributes. Consider the difference between the military hero and the military manager.

A good man isn't good for everything.

In communities where a coherent ruling group exists, the leading citizen can be thought of as having power in a generalized sense: he can bring about a change in zoning ordinances, influence the location of a new factory and determine whether the local museum will buy contemporary paintings. But in the dispersed and fragmented power system that prevails in the nation as a whole one cannot say, "So-and-so is powerful," without further elaboration. Those who know how our system works always want to know, "Powerful in what way? Powerful to accomplish what?" We have leaders in business and leaders in government, military leaders and educational leaders, leaders in labor and in agriculture, leaders in science, in the world of art and in many other special fields. As a rule, leaders in any one of these fields do not recognize the authority of leaders from a neighboring field. Often they don't even know one another, nor do they particularly want to. Mutual suspicion is just about as common as mutual respect—and a lot more common than mutual cooperation in manipulating society's levers.

All of this is directly at odds with the notion that our society is run by a coherent power group—the power elite, as C. Wright Mills called it, or the Establishment, as later writers have called it. It is hard not to believe that such a group exists. We want to believe that *someone* is minding the store.

Very few of our most prominent people take a really large view of the leadership assignment. Most of them are simply tending the machinery of that part of society to which they belong. The machinery may be a great corporation or a great government agency or a great law practice or a great university. They may tend it very well indeed, but they are not pursuing a vision of what the total society needs. They have not developed a strategy as to how it can be achieved, and they are not moving to accomplish it.

Scientific and professional people are accustomed to the kinds of problems that can be solved by expert technical advice or action. It is easy for them to imagine that any social enterprise could be managed in the same way. They envisage a world that does not need leaders, only experts. The notion is based, of course, on a false conception of the leader's function. The supplying of technically correct solutions is the least of his responsibilities.

People who have never exercised power have all kinds of curious ideas about it. The popular notion of leadership is a fantasy of capricious power. The top man presses a button and something remarkable happens. He gives an order as the whim strikes him, and it is obeyed.

The capricious use of power is relatively rare except in some large dictatorships and small family firms. Most leaders are hedged around by constraints—tradition, constitutional limitations, the realities of the external situation, rights and privileges of followers, the requirements of teamwork and, most of all, the inexorable demands of large-scale organization, which does not operate on capriciousness.

We are immunizing a high proportion of our most gifted young people against any tendencies to leadership. The

[127]

process is initiated by the society itself. The conditions of life in a modern, complex society are not conducive to the emergence of leaders. The young person today is acutely aware of the fact that he is an anonymous member of a mass society, an individual lost among millions of others. The processes by which leadership is exercised are not visible to him, and he is bound to believe they are exceedingly intricate. Very little in his experience encourages him to think he might someday exercise a role of leadership.

This unfocused discouragement is of little consequence compared with the expert dissuasion the young person will encounter if he is sufficiently bright to attend a college or university. In some institutions today the best students are carefully schooled to avoid leadership responsibilities.

Most of our intellectually gifted young people go from college directly into graduate school or into one of the older and more prestigious professional schools. There they are introduced to—or, more correctly, powerfully indoctrinated in—a set of attitudes appropriate to scholars, scientists and professional men. This is all to the good. The students learn to identify themselves strongly with their calling and its ideals. They acquire a conception of what a good scholar, scientist or professional man is like.

As things stand now, however, that conception leaves little room for leadership in the normal sense; the only kind of leadership encouraged is that which follows from the performing of purely professional tasks in a superior manner. Entry into what most of us would regard as the leadership roles in the society at large is discouraged.

In the early stages of a career there is a good reason for this: becoming a first-class scholar, scientist or professional requires single-minded dedication. Unfortunately, by the time the individual is sufficiently far along in his career to afford a broadening of interest, he often finds himself irrevocably set in a narrow mold.

The antileadership vaccine that the society administers to our young people today has other subtle and powerful ingredients. The image of the corporation president, politician or college president that is current among most intellectuals and professionals today has some decidedly unattractive features. It is said that such men compromise their convictions almost daily, if not hourly. It is said that they have tasted the corrupting experience of power. They must be status-seekers, the argument goes, or they would not be where they are.

Needless to say, the student picks up such attitudes. It is not that professors propound these views and students learn them. Rather, they are in the air and students absorb them. The resulting unfavorable image contrasts dramatically with the image these young people are given of the professional, who is almost by definition dedicated to his field, pure in his motives and unencumbered by worldly ambition.

My own extensive acquaintance with scholars and professionals on the one hand and administrators and managers on the other does not confirm this contrast in character. In my experience, each category has its share of opportunists. Nevertheless, the negative attitudes persist.

As a result the academic world appears to be approaching a point at which everyone will want to educate the technical expert who advises the leader, or the intellectual who stands off and criticizes the leader, but no one will want to educate the leader.

We have all seen men with lots of bright ideas but no patience with the machinery by which ideas are translated into action. As a rule, the machinery defeats them. It is a pity, because the professional and academic man can play a useful role in practical affairs. But too often he is a dilettante. He dips in here or there; he gives bits of advice on a dozen fronts; he never gets his hands dirty working with one piece of the social machinery until he knows it well. He will not take the time to understand the social institutions and processes by which change is accomplished.

The curse of citizen action is the glancing blow—a little work on this committee and on to the next one; a little work on that committee and on to something else. Too often the citizen active in community affairs is essentially a dabbler, never getting in deep enough to have any effect; never getting far enough below the surface to understand how the machinery works in whatever activity he is trying to change; just lingering long enough to sign the committee report, not staying long enough to see what the consequences of the report are.

That is not good enough in a society designed to depend on citizen concern and action.

We will never have effective leadership in our cities until we persuade the ablest and most influential members of the community that they must take personal responsibility for what happens to their city. It is one of the anomalies of our national life today that such persuasion is necessary. One might argue that when our ablest people evade the responsibility of leadership, the society is far gone in decadence. But we're not decadent. We're the victims of specialization. The able individual who doesn't lead is not just standing idle. He is a highly trained lawyer, busy pursuing his profession. Or a college professor busy writing books. Or a corporation executive busy with his business.

He has never been led to believe that the problems of the city are really his problems. But he must now learn that lesson. He must no longer believe that membership on the board of one distinguished hospital plus earnest participation in the Community Fund defines the limits of his civic duties. He must plunge with both feet into the city's toughest, grimiest and most complex problems, both short- and long-term: the question of today's riot and the question of whether the city itself has any tolerable future.

The plain fact is that all over this country today trouble is brewing and social evils accumulating while our patterns of social and professional organization keep able and gifted potential leaders on the sidelines.

Federal laws, dollars and programs don't teach children nor heal the sick. Teachers teach children and doctors heal the sick—individual teachers and doctors in the schools and clinics of Atlanta and Seattle and Phoenix. In other words, everything depends upon increased vitality out where the action is.

We must find ways of bringing together in some kind of working relationship the varied leadership elements in the community—the elected and appointed political leadership, business leaders, union leaders, educators, ministers, minority group leaders and the press.

What every city needs is a loose coalition of responsible leadership elements, willing to work together on a non-partisan basis to resolve urgent civic problems. I have watched many cities struggle with their problems, and I can assure you that such a coalition is necessary. City Hall can't go it alone. The business leaders can't go it alone. Minority leaders can't go it alone.

Of course, the coalition must be sufficiently fluid to permit the inclusion of all significant elements of community life; a coalition that excludes or suppresses important elements of potential community leadership is self-defeating.

One of the maladies of leadership today is a failure of confidence. Everyone who accomplishes anything of significance has more confidence than the facts would justify. It is something that outstanding executives have in common with gifted military commanders, brilliant political leaders and great artists. It is true of societies as well as of individuals. Every great civilization has been characterized by a sublime confidence in itself.

Lacking such confidence, too many leaders add ingenious new twists to the modern art which I call "How to reach a decision without really deciding." Require that the question be put through a series of clearances within your organization, and let the clearance process settle it. Or take a public-opinion poll and let the poll settle it. Or devise elaborate statistical systems, cost-accounting systems, information-processing systems, hoping that out of them will come unassailable support for one course of action rather than another.

19

The confidence required of leaders poses a delicate problem for a free society. We don't want to be led by Men of Destiny who think they know all the answers. Neither do we wish to be led by Nervous Nellies. It is a matter of balance. We are no longer in much danger, in this society, from Men of Destiny. But we *are* in danger of falling under the leadership of men who lack the confidence to lead. And we are in danger of destroying the effectiveness of those who have a natural gift for leadership.

We can have the kind of leaders we want, but we cannot choose to do without them. It is in the nature of social organization that we must have them at all levels of our national life, in and out of government—in business, labor, politics, education, science, the arts and every other field. Since we must have them, it helps considerably if they are gifted in the performance of their appointed task. The sad truth is that a great many of our organizations are badly managed or badly led. And because of that, people within those organizations are frustrated when they need not be frustrated. They are not helped when they could be helped. They are not given the opportunities to fulfill themselves that are clearly possible.

In the minds of some, leadership is associated with goals that they regard as distasteful—power, profit, efficiency and the like. But leadership, properly conceived, also serves the individual human goals that our society values so highly, and we shall not achieve those goals without it.

So much of our leadership energies have been devoted to tending the machinery and to keeping our complex society running that we have neglected even the possibility of moral leadership.

Leaders have a significant role in creating the state of mind that is the society. They can serve as symbols of the moral unity of the society. They can express the values that hold the society together. Most important, they can conceive and articulate goals that lift people out of their petty preoccupations, carry them above the conflicts that tear a society apart, and unite them in the pursuit of objectives worthy of their best efforts.

We don't need leaders to tell us what to do. That's not the American style of leadership in any case. We do need men and women in every community in the land who will accept a special responsibility to advance the public interest, root out corruption, combat injustice and care about the continued vitality of this land.

We need such people to help us clarify and define the choices before us.

We need them to symbolize and voice and confirm the most deeply rooted values of our society. We need them to tell us of our faithfulness or infidelity to those values.

And we need them to rekindle hope. So many of us are defeated people—whatever our level of affluence or status—defeated sometimes by life's blows, more often by our own laziness or cynicism or self-indulgence.

The first and last task of a leader is to keep hope alive—the hope that we can finally find our way through to a better world—despite the day's bitter discouragement, despite the perplexities of social action, despite our own inertness and shallowness and wavering resolve.

[134]

CHAPTER XXIII

DISPERSING

POWER AND INITIATIVE

IN RECENT DECADES, the American people have set themselves more and more goals that can be accomplished only through large expenditures of money and large-scale organization of effort. Some of these efforts—for example, national defense—are long-established. Some—for example, Social Security—have emerged in recent decades but are already firmly embedded in our national life. Some—for example, the space program—are new.

Such goals can be achieved only by harnessing vast resources of talent, money and organizational strength. That is one of the reasons we have moved, as every modern society must, toward larger and more comprehensive patterns of organization.

Not everyone is happy about all of the consequences of large-scale organization. But just about everyone covets the advantages that flow from it. It pays off heavily in benefits yielded for resources invested. For that reason business, government, labor, agriculture, the academic world, science and the professions have all been moving toward a society characterized by large-scale organization of effort.

The trend is evident in the fact that for thirty-five years the American people have moved consistently to expand the functions of the federal government. The American people are notably impatient and pragmatic. If they don't get what they want by one route, they try another route. If they had believed that they could achieve their shared goals within the old tradition of a weak federal government, no doubt they would have done so.

But we have a system characterized by the dispersion of power and initiative, and we like that attribute of the system. So we must develop means of mobilizing talent and resources that will move us toward our goals and at the same time will disperse power and initiative. Stated in simpler terms this means:

We must find far more effective ways of relating the federal government to state and local governments.

We must find new and better ways of involving private enterprise in the pursuit of social goals.

We must ask the universities to become even more deeply involved in carrying out public functions.

We must utilize increasingly a wide variety of nonprofit agencies in getting public work done.

And we must make certain that the relations between the federal government and all these other elements—state, local or private sector—are such as to preserve the integrity and vitality of the nonfederal partner. If we accomplish that, we will have resolved one of the central dilemmas of American political life. Despite the fact that they have for three decades acted to strengthen the federal establishment, the American people have never intended (and do not now intend) that their federal government should become all-powerful.

Nothing has changed more radically than the old argument between liberals who wanted a strong central government and conservatives who wanted a weak central government. (The conservatives talked states' rights, but they never promoted strong state and local government. They were essentially opposed to all government.)

Today the most intelligent liberals *and* conservatives favor strengthening state and local government, and call for creation of more flexible and effective federal-state-local partnerships. These partnerships cut across all the old arguments. They distribute power and initiative in new ways. They are beginning to be characterized by a new flexibility, a flexibility that frees state and local government to set its own goals and devise its own strategies.

The principles involved apply to the private sector as well. In our society a great deal of the potentiality for national accomplishment resides in the great estates of the private sector—industry, the universities, labor, the professions, agriculture, the press, foundations and other nonprofit organizations. The federal government must both seek their help and put itself at their disposal. It should use them and be used by them in the service of the shared goals of the American people.

The objective is a strong but not all-powerful federal government which relates itself in mutually respecting partnerships with state and local governments and with all the various elements of the private sector.

But is it really possible? "Partnership" is a word with a nice, warm glow to it, but can the federal government really share its power and initiative with state and local government? Can the federal government have a relationship with a university that does not subordinate the university?

These are questions that cannot be answered in generalities. In these matters the sooner we get beyond rhetoric the better. The heart of the matter is in the specific character of the relationships.

We must ask ourselves at every step how we can insure that state and local government will retain adequate autonomy and be capable of utilizing it. What conditions must surround the federal-state-local relationship if that is to occur?

If we want pluralism in the system (and I assume we do), we are going to have to build it in quite consciously and systematically. The logic of modern organization doesn't necessarily move us toward pluralism; in some cases it may move us away from it.

The ideas and practices involved in the new partnerships have deep roots in our national life. The idea of disciplined and mutually respecting relationships between the federal government and the states was built into our Constitution and our governmental structure. Voluntary and other non-governmental activity was already highly developed when De Tocqueville traveled here in 1835.

The first grants-in-aid to states were made in 1879. And Franklin Roosevelt used the general-welfare clause as grounds for greatly expanded grants to states in a time of national economic distress.

During World War II federal contract relationships with both industry and the universities were developed on an extensive scale.

Roughly three-fourths of the billion dollars spent annually by the National Institutes of Health is paid out on decisions made by *nongovernmental* scientists and citizens. It is an extraordinary partnership. Congress and the executive branch decide on the major fields of effort and levels of expenditure. NIH provides the administrative framework, creates the advisory groups and does the necessary staff work. But when the scientific proposals pour in from universities and laboratories all over the nation, the decisions are made by the outside advisers sitting on councils and committees.

In the light of this example it can be seen how inadequate are the old categories and clichés. Would a liberal or conservative find such arrangements more to his liking? The question has no relevance. Do the arrangements represent centralization or decentralization? Again, the categories are irrelevant. And there is no chapter in the textbooks on American Government that tells us how to think about such relationships.

The Medicare program, covering nineteen million older Americans, was shaped in complex collaboration between the federal government and the health professions, hospitals and nursing homes, Blue Cross–Blue Shield groups, commercial insurance carriers and others.

The first massive federal effort to assist local education, the Elementary and Secondary Education Act of 1965, recognizes the primacy of state and local authorities in the education of our children. The bulk of federal grants under the Act are made to state educational agencies, which in turn distribute the money to local school districts.

One of the most interesting examples of the government's relations with the private world involves those activities that are tax-exempt for educational, scientific, religious or charitable purposes. The implications of this tax exemption have not been well understood. The state is saying, in effect, that these activities are in the public interest, and, more important, that it is in the public interest to encourage the conduct of these activities by nongovernmental groups and individuals.

It would be difficult to exaggerate the importance of this policy in preserving and fostering the pluralism so characteristic of our society. The fact that our system encourages such diversity of initiative in the vitally important areas of education, science, religion and philanthropy has contributed to the richness and variety of our national life.

Much recent social legislation throws the challenge back to the local level to accomplish innovation. Consider the Economic Opportunity Act. It does not hand us a neat solution to poverty. It gives us authority and money to go out and look for a solution. It is a hunting license. It is a mandate to proceed with the difficult, exciting, painful process of social change. And the Office of Economic Opportunity has consistently thrown that challenge back to the local level.

Many other recent federal programs—for example, the Model Cities Program, Title III of the Elementary and Secondary Education Act, the Regional Medical Programs— follow the same tactic of inviting state and local governments to come up with the innovative efforts that the times require.

Reflecting on these examples, we can see how far we have moved beyond the unproductive clichés of the old liberal-conservative debate over the role of the federal government.

The important thing about the new approach is the idea of creative interplay between a responsible people and a responsive government. Like all other aspects of the American system it is open to continuous revision. If it doesn't work, we can and should improve it.

The relationship of the federal government to state and local government and to private groups will never be a comfortable one. The parties to the relationship have purposes that are overlapping but not identical. Each must play its role; each must be alert to preserve the integrity of its own purposes.

This comes out clearly in the relationship of the universities to the federal government. The universities have objectives that will never be fully shared (or perhaps even understood) by the federal government, and vice versa. The relationship will (and should) always be characterized by a certain wariness.

The partnership will never achieve its full potential if the nonfederal partner is weak or lacking in a sense of direction. The cities that have profited most strikingly from federal urban funds have been those in which local leadership and initiative were strong.

The partnership is similarly endangered if the federal partner is weak and faltering—for example, a weak regulatory agency dominated by those it seeks to regulate.

One could list a good many other requirements for a sound partnership: a clear definition of the relationship; open communication (including mutual criticism) between the two parties; orderly procedures for negotiation (including negotiation aimed at changing the ground rules of the relationship).

We must revitalize state and local leadership so that it can play its role vis-à-vis an increasingly powerful federal government without being completely submerged and obliterated. It is the only way to preserve our tradition of dispersed power and initiative. It is the only way to make workable the federal-state-local relationships we have been discussing.

We have a long tradition of weak and ineffective state and local government. There are impressive exceptions. But speaking generally, we combine a sentimental attachment to grass-roots democracy with an indolent cynicism about local government.

The weaknesses are legion: an inadequate tax structure;

archaic administrative machinery; mediocre personnel; fragmentation of function (health, welfare, etc.); officials who are not responsible or responsive to the governor or mayor; in the case of the city, splintered jurisdictions; in the case of the state, legislatures which themselves are ill-fitted for the modern world.

The system is too rickety to carry the heavy burdens we are now thrusting upon it.

The people themselves are going to have to take action to strengthen their local institutions.

And we won't make much headway until we get over our bad habit of looking down our nose at state and local politics. We have to begin to respect it in order to make it worthy of respect.

Young people who want to live lives of meaningful service —and there are more and more of them—should be encouraged to go into careers, elective or appointive, in state and local government. By doing so they will be on the moving frontier of American life. Nothing is more certain than that the next decade is going to see a drastic upgrading of state and local government.

Only then can we be assured of a society that is vital in all its parts, not just at the center but in every state and city, in every university and school district—a society that is responsive to its problems, capable of devising solutions and designed for flexible adjustment in form and practice.

That, in my opinion, is the only kind of society that stands a chance of survival in a swiftly changing and dangerous world, and the only kind of society in which individual freedom is likely to survive.

What is at stake is the future mode of organizing our society. It's worth our attention.

CHAPTER XXIV

THE INDIVIDUAL

AND SOCIETY

EVERYTHING about modern life seems to conspire against a sense of community, and as a result we have lost something that most of us need very much.

We need the stability that comes from a coherent community. We need the assurance of identity that comes from knowing and being known. We need the experience of a visible social context in which we fit. We need a sense of obligation to others. Perhaps more than anything else, we need a sense of participation.

Individuals actively participating in a community where they can see their problems face to face, know their leaders personally, sense the social structure of which they are a part—such individuals are the best possible guarantee that the intricately organized society we are heading into will not also be a dehumanized, depersonalized machine. They are also the best hope for curing the local apathy, corruption and slovenliness that make a mockery of self-government in so many localities.

The individual without roots, without a sense of identity or belonging, is a hazard to everyone, including himself. He is a ready recruit to strange causes. He is likely to lash out in desperate efforts to find meaning and purpose. We have too long pretended that people can live their lives without those ingredients. They cannot. And if they cannot find socially worthy meanings and purposes, they will cast about desperately and seize upon whatever comes to hand—extremist philosophies, nihilist politics, bizarre religions, far-out protest movements.

All that we know about the individual and society, and much that we know about the learning process, suggests that the individual actively participating is better than the individual inert or passive—a better learner, a better citizen, a more complete person, a more self-respecting individual.

Responsibility is the best of medicines. When people feel that important consequences (for themselves and others) hang on their acts, they are apt to act more wisely. It is not always easy to have that sense of responsibility toward a distant federal government. It helps if the ground on which responsibility is tested is at one's doorstep. Every man should be able to feel that there is a role for him in shaping his local institutions and local community.

We all know the symptoms that arise from failures in the relationship between the individual and society: feelings of alienation, anonymity, loss of identity, an oppressive sense of the impersonality of the society, a loss of any sense of participation or of any social context in which participation would have meaning.

Everyone has a different notion of who is at fault in the matter. The restless, middle-level industrial executive blames it on a corporate policy that creates "organization men." The young government worker blames it on the stupidity of the bureaucratic mind. The American student of the New Left blames it on capitalism. The Russian student thinks it must be some defect in the Communist system.

But they are all suffering from the same thing. It is a defect that characterizes all modern, large-scale social organizations.

This is a day of inner estrangement and outer conformity, and we must combat both.

At the same time that our intricately organized society is trying to bind the individual with the fetters of conformity, other circumstances of modern life are slicing through the moorings that relate the individual to his own tradition, to his own group and to the values which lie beyond the self. And unfortunately these latter relationships are precisely those which provide meaning and spiritual nourishment and a sense of identity. It is as though a deep-sea diver were to find himself being bound with more and more ropes to the mother ship, bound to the point where he could no longer move freely, and then to discover that his air hose had been snipped—all the freedom-limiting connections tightened and the life-giving connection severed.

We can't do without bigness in our organizations and institutions, but we can design them so that they serve the individual rather than the system. We can't avoid complexity, but we can organize the society so that individuals enjoy a sense of identity. Our goal should be a society designed for people; and if we want it badly enough, we can have it.

Institutions of whatever kind—and I mean hospitals and businesses and schools as well as governments—may be so constructed and so operated as to enhance *or* diminish the individual, to liberate him *or* smother him. We cannot exist without institutions; we cannot do the world's work or even live together without them. But we should never forget their central purpose in a free society.

Those who suffer from the sense of anonymity would feel better if they could believe that their society needed them. And the irony is that their society needs them desperately. But the need cannot be adequately expressed in rhetoric from Washington, nor can the invitation to lend a hand with the society's problems be effective until it is made real at the local level. That's the only level at which most people will ever be able to participate in any meaningful way.

That's why our goal must be a society that is vital in all its parts, in every state and city, in every university and school district, a society in which every individual feels that there is a role for him in shaping his local institutions and local community.

The man in the street thinks of freedom as the natural state, and lack of freedom as the unnatural, artificial, contrived state of affairs. He imagines that freedom, like sunshine or fresh air, is always there to be had if someone isn't forcibly preventing him from enjoying it. But freedom as we now know it has been exceedingly rare in the history of mankind. It is a highly perishable product of civilization, wholly dependent on certain habits of mind widely shared, on certain institutional arrangements widely agreed upon.

This is worth saying because some moderns are so enamored of the idea of individuality that they would not think of speaking out on behalf of society. They imagine that the only effect society can have on the individual is a destructive one. But it is by means of the free society that men keep themselves free. If men wish to remain free, they had better look to the health, the vigor, the viability of their free society.

In appraising the relation of the individual to society, we must arrive at a clear conception of the role of government. The purpose of government, first and last, must be to serve the individual. It is the instrument for achieving common goals that cannot be achieved by individuals. Few citizens understand this, and government rhetoric rarely clarifies it. The native canniness of the individual is not equal to the task of judging the safety of the drugs he buys or the planes he rides in. He must be served by regulatory agencies. Our great national parks and forests provide benefits that could not be had through individual action. Our postal system performs a service that can only be done nationally.

Our national problems have become so complex that it is not easy for the individual to see what he can do about them. The tasks facing the frontiersman two centuries ago may have been grim, but they were also obvious. Each man knew what he must do.

The whole society is becoming more elaborately articulated. This produces special kinds of strain in a society which seeks to preserve the autonomy and dignity of the individual. One middle-level executive said, "I don't mind the organization scratching my back for me. I do mind it telling me where I itch."

Too many of those who want to preserve freedom in an increasingly complicated world are affected with a crippling nostalgia. We cannot go back to a simpler world. We cannot escape complexity or large-scale organization or any of the other hallmarks of modern civilization. But we can make them serve the purposes of free men.

We now understand that we must free the individual and strengthen him, and *then* require that he be a responsible, mature and participating citizen. The paradigm is to be found in the rehabilitation of the physically handicapped. They need help and lots of it—for body, mind and spirit— but they also need to have the challenge thrown back to them to take a fiercely personal responsibility for their own recovery.

Just as the federal government must throw the challenge back to the local community, so must the society at every level throw the challenge back to the individual. But it must also serve and help the individual in many ways. No man is really free in any meaningful sense of the word without a certain modicum of security—of his person from violence, his conscience from coercion, his body from hunger and disease, his mind from fear for his own future and that of his children.

We are dedicated as a nation to providing those basic assurances, to those basic enlargements of human freedom.

We have outgrown the sink-or-swim individualism which assumed that all could and should compete equally in a battle for survival. We know now that many individuals need a lot of special help to free and strengthen them for full adult functioning.

But we have also outgrown the kind of paternalistic welfarism that creates self-perpetuating roles of dependence for many citizens.

That brings me to a word concerning the purpose of our efforts—the purpose of all our trials and errors and seeking and finding. It is to enhance the individual human being. That is easy to lose sight of because we talk, as we must, of institutions, of processes, of dollars. But their only legitimate purpose is to foster the conditions in which individual lives may be lived humanely.

It is not easy to live the good life in an enormously crowded and complicated world. A lot of rich as well as poor people find it increasingly hard to do so. When we look outward, we see complexity where we yearn for simplicity. When we look inward, all too often we see fragmentation when we long for wholeness.

The world *is* complex. We must accept that fact and learn to control it, so that as individuals we may be whole and not fragmented. We pass laws and design government programs to try to deal with complexity, to protect individuals from the buffeting of forces they cannot control. But we should never forget the central purpose of laws and government programs in a free society. That is to make the world manageable, so that individuals may have the maximum amount of freedom, freedom to grow and develop, freedom to be what they have it in them to be, freedom to choose.

No society can properly define for any individual the purpose and meaning of his life. The good society will create conditions in which the individual can find his own purpose and meaning in life.

CHAPTER XXV

ON AGING

Today there is a cruel and ironic contradiction in the fate of our older citizens. Never before have older people been able to look forward to so many years of vitality. But never before have they been so firmly shouldered out of every significant role in life—in the family, in the world of work and in the community.

The problem is heightened by the fact that most people, particularly men, find it virtually impossible to think realistically—or even to think at all—about their own retirement.

A man or woman of retirement age has four paramount problems to face.

One is income. The link between poverty and old age is an ancient one, and we have not completely broken it. Improvement in income levels, not only through pensions but through new employment opportunities, is critically important to a substantial proportion of our older people.

A second problem is health. The health problems of older

people are often inseparable from financial problems or problems caused by personal isolation.

A third problem is appropriate housing and living arrangements.

Fourth is interest and purpose in life. Older people differ not at all from their younger contemporaries in the requirement that life have some meaning.

We have made substantial progress in the first three of these areas in recent years. Virtually all older Americans now have some measure of Social Security coverage. It's still not adequate, but we're moving to improve it. The enactment of Medicare was truly a giant step. To provide more suitable housing for older people, we are moving toward patterns that include services and facilities to support independent living arrangements, personal-care homes, homes for the aged and nursing homes that are integrated with other community facilities.

The last of the four problems is often the least recognized and the most neglected. Yet it is at the heart of many of the difficulties of retirement.

One of the most useful things a society could do to help people adapt to retirement would be to give all its members in their early and middle years the kinds of experience that will build the capacity for self-renewal.

We all know people who retire psychologically when they are in their thirties or forties. They may continue working for another two or three decades, but psychologically speaking they have turned in their uniforms. Perhaps they just grew tired. Perhaps they were trapped by circumstance. Or perhaps they were defeated by self-doubt or fear or cynicism or self-indulgence.

In contrast, we all know people who at advanced ages retain an incredible freshness, curiosity, awareness and enthusiasm.

I do not believe we need to leave that outcome to chance. If we want to improve the quality of life for older people, we should do everything possible to increase the number of persons with the capacity for self-renewal.

Every institution in the society should work to that end. We are going to have to design our institutions so that they encourage continued learning and growth through in-service training, career-development programs, career counseling, systematic reassignment in the interest of growth, and sabbatical periods for study.

I would like to see the time come when many employing organizations will sponsor mid-career clinics to which men and women can go to re-examine the goals of their working lives and consider changes of direction. And I would like to see people visit such clinics with as little self-consciousness as they visit their dentist.

Too many middle-aged people are working at a fraction of full capacity because of circumstances that could be altered. Perhaps they are in a blind-alley job or a job unsuited to their talents, or caught in an unproductive relationship with their immediate supervisors. Perhaps they simply need challenge and change. Perhaps they are ready for a second career.

Whatever the problem, they need disinterested professional advice—and it is rarely available. They need counsel, and they need it under circumstances that will not impair their dignity or threaten their career investment. People in mid-career are apt to be quite sensitive about seeking help, and if the circumstances aren't right, they won't seek it.

Schools, universities, unions and other organizations could have similar clinics. Such clinics outside employing organizations would be sources of advice and guidance for the person contemplating a change of jobs or a geographical move. The clinics could have access through the U.S. Employment Service to nationwide information on job opportunities.

But what does all of this have to do with retirement? A great deal. If the individual reaching retirement is fully alive and accustomed to thinking constructively about life's transitions, he will be far better fitted for the next stage of the journey. Too often he is not. Too often he has learned no new skills or interests for years. Then we plunge him into one of life's toughest adjustments and expect him to make it easily.

Too many people face the retirement transition passively and fearfully, doing little to make it a constructive experience. But how could it be otherwise when many of them have spent the preceding years in circumstances that foster passivity?

Much has been said and written about the importance of preretirement information and counseling. The first objective of such counseling seems childishly simple but is really quite difficult: to persuade the individual to *think* about his own future. One would suppose that it would be easy and natural for middle-aged people to think about the years ahead, but in most cases their reluctance to do so is beyond belief.

During the first twenty-five years, life in this country is so future-oriented that for many of our young people the present has little reality. They live with their eye on the upward curve of their own careers and fortunes. Only the future is real. Then in middle life the future vanishes.

In considering retirement itself, we must deal first with one of the most widely debated questions of all: Is it unnecessarily rigid for organizations to have a fixed retirement age for everyone?

A fixed chronological age for retirement is the predominant practice today. Its chief justification is that it avoids the difficult problem of individualized judgments on each case.

But it has been argued that people age at strikingly different rates, and that this should be taken into account. The argument is not without merit. It is conceivable that we could develop physiological and psychological measures of aging that would be far more precise than chronological age in identifying the appropriate moment for retirement.

Unfortunately, there are two difficulties. One is that individualized retirement judgments wouldn't necessarily meet one of the prime reasons for a fixed retirement age, namely, to make room for younger people.

The second difficulty is that retirement based on individualized measures of physiological and psychological aging might be unnecessarily cruel to those who failed the test. They would be handed a certified assurance of uselessness.

Nevertheless, many improvements on present practices are possible. For example, other professions might profitably study the civilized practices common among law firms. Many firms have arrangements to make it possible for an elderly partner to continue in some meaningful relationship to the firm and its work.

More and more organizations are beginning to make special provisions for phasing the period of retirement, for hiring retired people from other organizations, or rehiring their own retirees under special arrangements. This practice is especially common now in the academic world, where able professors are beginning to enjoy a postretirement market for their skills.

Some have suggested that formal retirement would be less traumatic and the whole life cycle more rational if we thought of every career as having three components: study, work and community service. The weights accorded each component would vary from one individual to another, and would change as the years pass. Under ideal conditions, the study component would be dominant in the early years of life, tapering off for most people during the twenties and thirties, rising briefly perhaps for a period of mid-career training and rising markedly in retirement years for those who would enjoy further formal or informal education. The work component would build up to a dominant level in early and middle maturity and drop off for most people in later years. The community service component might have an early peak (for example, a tour of duty in the Peace Corps), but would normally begin to rise during mature years. And this component might well reach a peak during the retirement years.

[158]

That is an oversimplified model, but the principle is an interesting one.

Older people, like all others, vary greatly in their desires, interests and needs, and we should not presume to judge what will be best for them.

Some will want to work until the day they drop; others will want to pitch horseshoes; others will want to watch someone else pitch horseshoes.

Some will want to be part of a community; others will want to be alone.

Some will want to remain in their own town; others will want to be foot-loose.

So we must design a society in which older people have choices. And in designing such a society, we shall have to work harder on some choices than on others. It's already fairly easy for the older person to be alone; it is often much harder for him to find companionship and friends. It's already easy for him to find a park bench to sit on; it is much harder for him to find useful work.

Despite a good deal of progress in recent years, one of the most serious defects in our present arrangements for older people is the absence of relevant and useful things for them to do, whether this be paid work or a personal activity. Like everyone else, older people need to be needed. They need to have something to occupy their hands and minds and hearts.

In our society, this range of needs is generally supplied by work. A job has meaning beyond the salary received. It is a social environment, a source of friends, a supplier of purpose. How much of life's fullness disappears when the job disappears is one of the tragic surprises of retirement.

[159]

But for the retired person, work is often hard to obtain. We need far more imaginative attempts to supply work opportunities for retired people, including part-time jobs. The latter are especially important since the retired person often has many reasons for wanting to work less than full time.

Opportunities to remain active are not confined to conventional employment. The Foster Grandparent and Green Thumb programs provide significant opportunities that serve all the purposes of meaningful work. We have barely begun to scratch the surface of such possibilities. It would be possible to develop a considerable variety of activities patterned after the Peace Corps and VISTA that would serve the community and give older citizens something significant to do. Again, such activities should be made possible on a part-time as well as full-time basis.

The possibilities are limitless because of the serious shortages in every one of the so-called helping professions. If you set yourself the task of identifying those fields of human activity that cannot be automated—the areas in which humans cannot be replaced by machines—you will find that many involve the helping fields. You can automate some of the activities a nurse performs, but the human element is of the essence. The usefulness of a companion to an elderly person is not just in the tasks performed but in the human interaction.

Our arrangements for bringing together people who need help and people who want to be helpful are still rudimentary. An elderly lady living on the fifth floor of a large urban apartment house may need companionship in the worst way, and another, more vigorous older lady living on the seventh floor may need to be needed. We haven't yet been sufficiently inventive in the ways of bringing them together.

There is no reason why a considerable variety of groups—clubs, unions, fraternal organizations—shouldn't design their own "helping" corps of older people for volunteer work in a local setting.

I would like to see this helping principle applied to a whole town. I would like to see some community say: "Within our city limits no child who needs a tutor will lack one, no hospital will lack nurses' aides, no social agency will lack volunteers," and so on. Then I would like to see that community organize to meet its commitment. In such a community every person with willing hands and a willing heart would be a needed and valued participant, whatever his age.

I hope that the next few years will bring greater attention and thought to the value and meaning of leisure, and the wise use of leisure in our society. I believe that we are already gaining some wisdom in this matter. Leisure is no longer thought of as simply unfilled time or thumb-twiddling (though no one, in a world full of terrifying action, should downgrade thumb-twiddling). It is beginning to be viewed as an opportunity for all kinds of activities that contribute to individual growth, enrichment and satisfaction.

But though retirement holds opportunity for new experience and growth, it would be wrong to suggest that the new will predominate, even for the most adventurous older people. The meaning in their lives is already deeply and irrevocably associated with certain places, people, organizations and communities—and they will probably be wise to retain some if not all of those associations.

That is why we must design our arrangements for older people in such a way that those who wish it can be near their families rather than in some distant housing project for the elderly, and those who wish it can remain in their own neighborhood rather than migrate to some "retirement community." And that is why it is useful for companies and unions to have retirement clubs and communities and other arrangements to permit continuing identification by the older person with the world he belongs to and knows best.

CHAPTER XXVI

MISCELLANY

Take the statistical view of rascals and fools. There are so many per thousand in the population. You have to meet your share.

If you seem to be meeting more than your share, lie down: you may be tired.

When I say that we must look to the future rather than the past, I'm not suggesting that we should not revere our ancestors. Heaven forbid. The nearer I get to being one, the more reverent I feel.

Don't let anyone talk to me about the good old days. To me one of the characteristics of the good old days was an almost unlimited capacity to tolerate social injustice.

Some people tell me that in the good old days every family took care of its own aged and somehow that was better and healthier all around.

A more honest account would make some reference to the

number of older people who, in the phrase of those good old days, went "over the hill to the poorhouse."

A more honest account would make some reference to the old people who were mendicants within their own families and were pretty much at the mercy of their relatives.

A more honest account would make some reference to the hypocrisy which made it possible for us to neglect our older people for so many years and to commit the injustices which we are now trying to correct.

In framing federal programs, we must beware of the old American habit of spending dollars to still our anxieties. An anthropologist friend of mine who lived in the Southwest said of the traditional Indian rain dance, "The dance didn't bring rain, but it made the tribe feel a lot better." So it is with some of our federal spending.

Anyone who wishes to make moral sense out of his life must recognize from the first that he is undertaking the venture in a world that often fails to appreciate moral sense and usually practices moral nonsense. In other words, it is his own project; he cannot make it dependent upon whether his neighbor does likewise.

The man who says "I have no illusions" is suffering from the gravest illusion of all.

It may seem paradoxical, but if you have some respect for people as they are, you can be more effective in helping them to become better than they are.

As the alcoholic seeks a drink, the inveterate hater seeks an object—any object—on which to vent his animosity.

Some people enjoy punishing others and look forward to transgressions that justify it. If the transgressions don't occur readily, such people will often invent or invite them.

Everyone has an inalienable right to waste his talent if he wishes.

I am not one of those who believe that a goal is somehow unworthy if everyone can achieve it.

You will never advance far in your understanding of another culture if you devote yourself to exclaiming that some things about it are wonderful and other things are terrible. This comes under the heading of entertainment and should not be confused with understanding. No society is all good or all bad, and the discovery that any particular society is compounded of both good and bad is not a very impressive finding. What you must try to do is to understand what problems a society faces; why it has developed the way it has; why it has certain characteristics rather than others; why it does some things so well and other things very badly.

The greatest psychotherapeutic medicine we know anything about is sleep. When your prevailing mood becomes one of anxiety or fear or hostility or misery, take the medicine! Sleep!

Specialization and division of labor are at the heart of modern organization. In this connection I always recall a Marx Brothers movie in which Groucho played a shyster lawyer. When a client commented on the dozens of flies buzzing around his broken-down office, Groucho said, "We have a working agreement with them. They don't practice law and we don't climb the walls."

I am all for professionals. They have created the modern world—but I don't hold that against them.

When events push a fellow worker momentarily off balance, when anxiety and fatigue undermine his judgment, don't punish him for his errors. Restore him.

It is not easy for any of us to bear in mind that the free society is still the exceptional society. The ideal of a free society is still unattainable or unacceptable to most of the world's peoples. Many live under governments which have no inclination to foster freedom. Others are hemmed in by their own ignorance or by rigid social stratification. The foes of freedom are still ready to argue that the unruliness, sloth and self-indulgence of men make a free society simply impractical. The world is full of people who believe that men need masters.

Social criticism has its fashions. Everyone who can spell the word "conformity" is writing a book about it. To attack conformity is the latest way to conform. And social critics assail TV and Madison Avenue the way athletes do push-ups and knee bends—not with profound purpose but just to get their blood circulating.

Abraham Flexner, who wrote the report that revolutionized American medical education, was entirely without the obvious qualification of a medical background. All that he had was a razor-edged mind, fierce integrity, limitless courage and the capacity to express himself clearly and vividly. And that proved to be enough.

The most interesting subject of study is man, the light-skulled, inventive, communicative creature who builds great civilizations and destroys them.

Whatever difficulties democracy may be having in the world as a going way of life, it is having no trouble in getting lip service from nearly everyone.

The question for our society is not whether we are better than we used to be. The question is whether we are good enough.

Moral seriousness does not resolve complex problems; it only impels us to face the problems rather than run away. Clearheadedness does not slay dragons; it only spares us the indignity of fighting paper dragons while the real ones are breathing down our necks. But those are not trivial advantages.

CHAPTER XXVII

HAZARD AND HOPE

THE PROSPECTS never looked brighter and the problems never looked tougher. Anyone who isn't stirred by both of those statements is too tired to be of much use to us in the days ahead.

It isn't a naturally just, or kindly, or friendly, or orderly world. It never was. It never will be.

In some communities and nations, at some moments in history, men have succeeded in creating social institutions and traditions that temper the natural ferocity of the species. But only with difficulty and only through unceasing effort.

To the extent that the ideals of freedom, justice, brotherhood and individual fulfillment have been extended and made real, it has happened because some men and women have had the irrepressible conviction that betterment of the human condition is possible.

There will never be a time when mankind is not in imminent danger. Cruelty, violence and brutality will be held in leash only by unceasing effort—if held in leash at all. Sloth, indulgence, smugness, torpor begotten of ease and flabbiness born of security will always lurk in wait. Rigidity, emptiness of spirit, narrow conventionality and stuffed-shirtism are diseases that may attack any society. No society will ever solve the issue of the individual versus the organization. No society will ever discover how to become civilized without running the risk of becoming overcivilized. No society will ever resolve the tension between equality and excellence.

History never looks like history when you are living through it. It always looks confusing and messy, and it always feels uncomfortable.

It is an abiding characteristic of man to believe that the old virtues are disappearing, the old values disintegrating, the old, good, stern ways no longer honored. Many people today seem to think that our values, our morality as a people, our devotion to virtue and justice resemble a reservoir that was filled long ago (vaguely, about the time of our grandfathers) and has been seeping away ever since. But our grandfathers thought that the reservoir had been filled by *their* grandfathers and had been seeping away ever since.

It does not surprise me that many young people think of the moral order as something invented by parents, deans and commencement speakers for the sole purpose of boring the young. We give them the impression that their task is to stand a dreary watch over the ancient values, when we should be telling them the grim but bracing truth that it is their task to re-create those values continuously in their own behavior, facing the dilemmas and catastrophes of their own time. We give them the impression that the ideals we cherish are safely embalmed in the memory of old battles and ancestral deeds, when we should be telling them that each generation refights the crucial battles, and either brings new vitality to the ideals or allows them to decay.

The capacity of our people to believe stubbornly and irrepressibly that this is a world worth saving, and that intelligence and energy and goodwill may save it, is one of the most endearing and bracing of American traits.

No sensible person relishes the immature aspects of our optimism, but if we lose that optimism we will surely be a less spirited people, a less magnanimous people and an immeasurably less venturesome people. Zest and generosity will disappear from our national style. And our impact on the world may well disappear along with them.

If a society believes that its institutional arrangements are no longer capable of translating its ideals into practice, trouble is on the way. Of course, ideal and reality never fuse. But that is not fatal if the members of the society believe that some kind of confrontation between ideal and reality is possible, and that plans are afoot to narrow the gap. If they do not believe either of those things, they will either rebel or sink into the hopeless and cynical passivity of many older societies.

Today the first duty of responsible citizens is to bind together rather than tear apart. The fissures in our society are already dangerously deep. We need greater emphasis on the values that bind us together. And I don't just mean between Negro and white, or between rich and poor, but between conservative and liberal, Democrat and Republican, labor and management, North and South.

We need a greater common allegiance to the goals and binding values of the national community.

Responsible citizens concerned to make this a better society have to cope with two contrasting attitudes on the part of their fellow citizens.

One is a violent, explosive impatience to get it all done instantly—and bitter disillusionment if that doesn't happen.

The other is a disinclination to take any action at all—sometimes from disagreement with objectives, more often from apathy or cynicism. "You can't really change anything," the worldling tells us. "Live with the world's limitations."

Both attitudes pose serious threats. We can be brought down by the volatility of our aspirations or by our incapacity to aspire.

I believe that Americans today have no less moral fiber than they did a generation ago. After all, I'm old enough to remember the Flapper Era, which was not morally fibrous.

There is something disheartening about the modern scene —the confusion, the disorder, the changing values, the constant push-and-pull of conflict, the vastness and impersonality of the systems that govern our lives.

But at the same time the possibilities of an improved life for mankind are more exciting than ever in the long history of the race. We hold in our hands the tools to build the kind of society our forebears could only dream of. If ever a generation of Americans has found the moral equivalent of war that William James called for, it is this generation.

We can lengthen the life span, as they could not. We can feed our children better and educate them better. We can communicate better among ourselves and with all the world.

We have the technology and the means of advancing that technology. We have the intellectual talent and the institutions to develop it and liberate it. We have, or we can build, the systems and organizations, public and private, through which our common goals can be pursued.

We have these things not because we are any smarter than those who came before us but because we can build cumulatively on their creative effort and achievements.

Far less than any other generation in the history of man are we the pawns of nature, of circumstance and of uncontrollable forces—unless we make ourselves so.

We built this complex, dynamic society, and we can make it serve our purposes. We designed this technological civilization, and we can manage it for our own benefit. If we can build organizations, we can make them serve the individual.

To do this takes a commitment of mind and heart—as it always did. If we make that commitment, this society will more and more come to be what it was always meant to be: a fit place for the human being to grow and flourish.

INDEX